Schooners in Four Centuries

An unforgettable sight in the harbour of Port St Mary, Isle of Man, as six schooners sit on the bottom in a few feet of water drying their sails in the light breeze. On the left is the **Margaret Garton** built at the port in 1877 of 52 tons, and directly astern of her and in the centre of the picture is another two-master, the **Venus** of Castleton, built at Perth in 1876 of 72 tons. *(David Clement Collection)*.

Schooners in Four Centuries

David R. MacGregor

NAVAL INSTITUTE PRESS

Published and distributed in the United States
of America and Canada by the Naval Institute
Press, Annapolis, Maryland 21402

Library of Congress Catalog Card No. 82-73779.
ISBN 0-87021-958-8
First published 1982.

Phototypeset by Grange Filmsetting Birmingham.
Printed and bound by Mackays of Chatham Ltd.

Designed by Kaye Bellman

To Margaret and Donald Francke

Larger scale copies of the plans
reproduced in this book can
be obtained on application to the Author.

By the same Author:
The Tea Clippers (1952, reprinted 1972).
The China Bird (1961).
Fast Sailing Ships 1775-1875 (1973).
Square Rigged Sailing Ships (1977).
Clipper Ships (1979).
Merchant Sailing Ships 1775-1815 (1980).

Contents

Purely fore-and-aft schooners were rare in Great Britain on commercial craft whereas in the United States the reverse was the case after the 1850s and square sails became a rare exception. Here the Mary Langdon of Rockland, Maine, (built at Thomaston in 1845 of 91 tons and rebuilt in 1860) presents a different profile to her British counterpart: two large deckhouses; boat on stern davits; different shaped stern; wooden balustrade up to fore rigging because deck was level with main rail; 'lazy jacks' on mainsail to prevent sail spilling on to deck when being lowered. These American wooden schooners were broader in proportion to length, the Mary Langdon having a length of 73 feet equal to only $3\frac{1}{2}$ breadths. [PEABODY MUSEUM, SALEM]

Introduction

There are often chapters about schooners in books on the sea but they do not often get a complete book to themselves which is surprising considering the vast numbers that have been built and the numerous purposes to which they have been put. Perhaps it is this very wide-ranging use of the word 'schooner' which defies a quick and easy recognition of their activities. When writing about square-riggers, one usually is not obliged to include examples of other rigs to elucidate one's point, but schooners have been so many things over the centuries and have even carried so many rig-combinations that it becomes no easy task to describe them succinctly.

In the study of living vessels or of ones whose bones still exist to haunt our imagination, I have found that personal contact with the men who sailed on them is of great value. Also important have been the expeditions to measure and study the survivors. It was in 1948 that Basil Greenhill first introduced me to Appledore and extolled the beauty of the schooner, ketch and trading smack and the part they played in maritime development. Together we visited several ports and sites in the West Country as well as in Scandinavia. I recall other expeditions made with the late Oliver H. Hill and the late Vernon Boyle when heavily-engined ketches and schooners still traded to north Devon ports. More recently I have been on several expeditions with Ralph Bird to measure and examine old hulks and I am grateful to him for the new sources of information he has generously provided.

In the first two-and-a-half centuries covered by this book there were no cameras to take pictures of schooners, and artists often ignored vessels of this category, but in the last hundred years or more photographers have recorded schooners and so it is inevitable that the majority of the illustrations cover the period since 1850 in greater detail than for previous years. In addition, the schooner did not develop to any great extent in most countries until after 1835 or so with the result that the invention of photography fortuitously coincides with the increasing popularity of the schooner.

An attempt has been made to use new photographs or other illustrations or at least ones that have not been reproduced too much, and in this context I should like to acknowledge the assistance given by several people. In this country, David Clement generously placed his collection at my disposal and as a result several new photographs have emerged including the splendid one forming the title page. He took a great deal of trouble in copying contact prints made by W. A. Sharman from his own negatives or other prints collected by Sharman. In Denmark, Frode Holm-Petersen, whom I have known for over thirty years, has greatly assisted me with Danish vessels. In the United States of America, Karl Kortum, Director of the San Francisco

Maritime Museum, has given generously of his advice and looked out useful pictures for me; his grasp on all maritime matters is immense and results in original thinking on well-known topics. Also in California, Robert Weinstein gave me full access to his large collection of photographs.

Obsessed as I have been with the study of hull-form, I must mention the late Howard I. Chapelle who steered me along in the study of Baltimore clippers and other schooners built for speed on both sides of the Atlantic.

Other friends who assisted my researches on the north American continent have been John S. Carter, Curator of Maritime History at the Peabody Museum, Salem, who gave me full access to the photographic records and assisted me in other ways; Captain W. J. Lewis Parker who sent me a selection of photographs of the larger schooners; Dr. Charles A. Armour of Halifax, Nova Scotia, also sent me a selection of Canadian schooner photographs to choose from; also my thanks to Andrew Nesdall for his comments; and finally to John Shedd of Model Shipways, Bogota, New Jersey, for permission to reproduce so many of their sail plans.

In Great Britain I should like to record my thanks to the staff in the Print Room of the National Maritime Museum and especially to George A. Osbon who was in charge of the photographic collection for many years; to Bertram Newbury of the Parker Gallery for allowing me to browse through their files; and to James Henderson for help with Aberdeen schooners. Other collections made available to me over the years were those of the late Richard Gillis and the late W. J. Cock. Some acknowledgements have been given according to the information written on the photograph when the latter has been found in an album or purchased in a shop. Of course I have been an avid collector myself for many years, always looking for new examples of illustrative material.

In the matter of coyping old photographs, some I have done myself and others have been copied by George Weston to whom I offer my sincere thanks for all his trouble and patience.

David R. MacGregor
Barnes, London, 1982

CHAPTER ONE

Definitions

Small boat handling is practised by many today and gives a thrill because of the direct contact with the wind and water, which can be achieved by means of a simple form of rig. A schooner is basically such a simple form, especially in its first century of use or as used in shallops, and provides an effective use of wind power as a means of propulsion needing only a small crew to handle it. Square-rigged vessels, by contrast, require a more complicated system of rigging to control and operate the sails and thus need larger crews. Nevertheless, the three-masted square-rigged ship had been in use for some two centuries before the forerunner of the schooner appeared on the scene.

It was the square sail, lug sail and spritsail which were commonly in use in northern Europe in the sixteenth century, and it was the last two that could be handled by the least number of men and which performed best in working to windward. All these

French fishing boats carrying lugsails on three masts; the upper sails were used in regattas, the top gallant sails were probably confined to regattas. [MacGREGOR COLLECTION].

sails were four-sided, but whereas the square sail and lug hung from a spar called a 'yard', the spritsail—as its name implies—had a spar called a 'sprit' to hold up its peak. Basically a gaff sail was the same shape as a spritsail with the sprit omitted but with a spar called a 'gaff' supporting the 'head' or upper edge of the sail and pivoted on the mast. The earliest gaff sails, however, had very short gaffs according to seventeenth century pictures.

In *Man on the Ocean* (1874), R. M. Ballantyne describes 'The Schooner' in these words:

'This is the most elegant and, for small craft, the most manageable vessel that floats. Its proportions are more agreeable to the eye than those of any other species of craft, and its rig is in favour with owners of yachts—especially with those whose yachts are large. The schooner's distinctive peculiarities are, that it carries two masts, which usually "rake aft" or lean back a good deal; and its rig is chiefly fore-and-aft, like the sloop. Of the two masts, the *after* one is the *main-mast*. The other is termed the *fore-mast*. The sails of a schooner are—the *main-sail* and *gaff* [*topsail*] on the *main-mast*; the *fore-sail*, *fore-top-sail*, and *fore-top-gallant-sail* (the two last being square sails), on the fore-mast. In front of the fore-mast are the *stay-sail*, the *jib*, and the

Another form of fore-and-aft rig was the ketch, and here one is seen under full sail 'coming up the narrows' to Padstow. The mizen is a shorter mast than the main but it carries a similar form of gaff sail; it is also a pole mast without a fidded topmast. The main topsail has a head yard. [RICHARD GILLIS COLLECTION].

In Penzance Harbour at low water three classic forms of rig lie side-by-side. From left to right they are a brigantine, a cutter and a two-masted schooner, the bow of which has been cut off by the photographer. The schooner is the conventional British kind with square topsails on the foremast. The cutter sets the same form of gaff sail as found on both the schooner and on the mainmast of the brigantine. [F. E. GIBSON].

flying-jib; these last are triangular sails . . . Schooners sometimes carry a large square-sail, which is spread when the wind is "dead aft". They are much used in the coasting trade; and one of their great advantages is that they can be worked with fewer "hands" than sloops of the same size.'

Of course, schooners can have two or more masts but there must be a gaff sail on each mast and this should be the principal sail on that mast. The same sort of gaff sails given to schooners can also be found on the sloop, ketch, brigantine, barquentine and even a barque, especially a three-masted one. Some ketches were larger than schooners and proved a more economical form of rig. Leg-of-mutton or Bermuda sails were uncommon on trading schooners after 1815.

Schooners were used mainly for pleasure in their earliest forms but since 1700 have carried every conceivable cargo; have been employed in estuaries, coastal work and ocean voyages; they have been humble carriers or smart clippers, privateers or slavers, fishermen, pilots or school ships. Examples of most types are given here. However, there is insufficient space to explore deeply into any one vessel; and so this will be a broad and general survey.

This model of the three-masted schooner Alert, *presumably the one built at Runcorn in 1885, shows the ratio of hull to mast height that was normal in the nineteenth and twentieth centuries. It also shows the yards carried by British and many European schooners on the foremast. As no sails are set, the three gaffs are lowered, but as some of the running rigging is in white thread on the model, it has disappeared on the photograph.* [PARKER GALLERY].

A British two-masted schooner sailing quietly out of Fowey harbour under full sail. She carries the typical canvas for her rig although her square fore topgallant has been replaced by two triangular ones. [OSBORNE STUDIOS].

Two-masted Boats

Although the word 'schooner' is attributed first to a chance remark by a spectator at the launch of a two-masted vessel in New England in about 1713, other craft with similar arrangements of fore-and-aft sails had existed in various forms for over a century. The earliest known illustration appears to be an ink drawing by the Dutch artist Rool dated 1600 in which the Burgomasters of Amsterdam are disporting themselves on their yacht, which is running before the wind goosewinged, with her sails boomed out on opposite sides. There is a 'shoulder of mutton' sail with a very short gaff set on each mast; the mainsail on the taller mast is much larger than the foresail and the foremast is stepped right up in the eyes of the boat; there is no bowsprit and no jib. The leeboard on the port side is drawn hauled up and the sheer sweeps up to a high stern. This illustration was reproduced in Arthur H. Clark's *History of Yachting* (1904).

In the same book, Clark has an engraving of a dozen or so such craft greeting Queen Mary of France at Amsterdam in 1638 and each firing a bow gun in salute. Other similar illustrations exist, including Hartgers' view of New Amsterdam (New York) drawn about 1627 and a painting by Adam Willaerts of Batavia harbour in 1649. There is evidence, William A. Baker tells us in his book *Sloops & Shallops*, that such vessels carried a bowsprit and triangular headsail by about 1650.

The Dutch employed the word *jaght* to define a craft built to sail swiftly and of light construction whether it was for merchant or naval purposes. Their Admiralty yachts and their State yachts, which acted in the same way as Revenue Cutters did in England, carried a single gaff sail or spritsail together with a bowsprit supporting two headsails, and there was sometimes a square topsail. Some hulls went up to 70 feet in length. In England, the word 'yacht' was corrupted to mean any craft used for pleasure. The Dutch used the term *speeljaght* for a pleasure craft and these were generally two-masted and of the kind already described with their shoulder-of-mutton sails. Illustrations depict them in harbours or estuaries and so they were probably not more than about 35 feet in length.

In the seventeenth century two-masted boats of this kind would have been classed as 'sloops' from the Dutch word *sloepe*. Thomas Blanckley's celebrated definition of this word in his *Naval Expositor* compiled in 1732, allots sloops one, two or three masts, square or round sterns, and capable of setting the following sails: Bermuda, shoulder-of-mutton, square, lug or smack—the last presumably meaning gaff rather than spritsail.

By 1700 there appears to have been little change in the two-masted rig, although

A Dutch speeljaght *painted by Simon de Vlieger (1600-53) with short gaffs and high ornamented stern. There are no shrouds and the leeboard is hauled up.* [RUPERT PRESTON GALLERY].

The mezzotint referred to as published in the Mariner's Mirror *(vol. I) was possibly made from this painting, attributed to Van de Velde the younger. At least they are broadly similar, but this illustration shows the rigging, sails, flags and hulls quite clearly and distinctly. Two schooners are here, each with a headsail on a bowsprit. On the left is a typical cutter with an elaborately carved stern and her mainsail brailed in. The schooner in the foreground has a broadside of six guns.* [PARKER GALLERY].

the bowsprit and jib were now established and craft of larger size were obviously constructed. Arthur H. Clark quotes from a marine dictionary published at Amsterdam in 1702 which lists dimensions of a two-masted sloop 42 feet long and 9 feet broad; the stem was $5\frac{1}{2}$ feet high, the sternpost was 7 feet high and raked 2 feet aft. Dimensions of the masts were as follows: foremast 15 feet, fore gaff 10 feet, fore boom $11\frac{1}{2}$ feet; mainmast 24 feet, main gaff $12\frac{1}{2}$ feet, main boom 21 feet.

One of these two-masted sloops is illustrated in volume I of the *Mariner's Mirror*, being taken from an undated Van de Velde painting, but it must be prior to 1707 when the younger artist of that name died. The vessel is flying English colours and has a broadside of five guns. The mainsail is much larger than the foresail and there is a bowsprit and headsail.

So the rig was obviously being copied and used in England as was only natural considering the close trade links and proximity of the two coastlines. A large example was the *Royal Transport* of 220 tons, carrying 20 guns and a crew of 100 men which was launched at Chatham in 1695 and given by William III to Peter the Great two years later.

An interesting survival of the seventeenth century rig of the two-masted boat without a headsail may be had in the Block Island boats as recounted by E. P. Morris in *The Fore-and-Aft Rig in America*. There were sixty such craft in 1883 but they had all vanished by 1925 with the exception of a full-size replica. They were double-ended craft intended to be launched from a beach, yet they had a 'V' bottom; length varied from 18 to 26 feet. Block Island lies off the coast of Rhode Island.

Of course, during the seventeenth century a more common form of two-masted rig, to judge by surviving paintings, was the square-rigged ketch with yards on both masts, and a number were in use in England; there was also the brigantine.

CHAPTER THREE

Colonial America

Two-masted vessels rigged with lateen yards on each mast are pictured in panoramic views of New York harbour in the second half of the seventeenth century, but after 1700 the lateen only appears as a mizen, it having been superseded by the gaff. This applies to views of both New York and New England. As regards illustrations of the gaff rig, William Burgis' view of New York (1717), has many three-masted square-rigged ships and also numerous single-masted craft with gaff sails but apparently no fore-and-aft two-masters. None of the cutters appears to carry a square topsail, not even the largest which mounts a broadside of five guns, and some of them have quite short gaffs. There is one two-master rigged down to the lower masts which are of equal height and with her yards lowered on the lifts; there is also the mastless hulk of a two-master with a tall flag pole set up amidships.

But in his 1725 view of Boston, William Burgis has drawn a much greater variety of craft. In addition to the many three-masted square-rigged ships, there are two brigantines in the modern sense of the word with two square sails on the foremast and a large gaff mainsail; there is a ketch, square-rigged on the mainmast and with a lateen on the mizen; there are many single-masted craft, of which certainly two carry two yards on a tall mast; and there are also four two-masters, two of which are undoubtedly gaff-rigged on each mast. One of the latter is under sail with a single headsail; the other at anchor has two stays from foremast to bowsprit, the gaff sails being triced up with the clew hauled out to the boom end.

It was in the seaport of Gloucester, Massachusetts, that the story originated of who first invented the schooner. According to tradition it occurred about 1713 when Andrew Robinson was launching a new vessel and upon her entering the water, a spectator called out, 'Oh, how she scoons!', whereupon Robinson remarked: 'A scooner let her be'.

Writing in 1904, Arthur H. Clark said that no marine use of the word 'scooner' had been found prior to 1713, and he cited the derivation of the word from the Dutch 'schoon', taken from a Dutch-Latin dictionary published in 1599, meaning 'beautiful, fair, lovely'. He added that in thirteen applications given in the dictionary for the use of the word, not one had a nautical connotation. Just as in the case of coining the word 'clipper' for a fast-sailing ship, its use having been applied to horses, so 'scoons' need have had no maritime background. E. P. Morris's conclusion in 1927 was that the story 'is nothing more than a picturesque adornment of the Gloucester tradition'.

In any case, there is sufficient evidence to prove that vessels of this rig had already

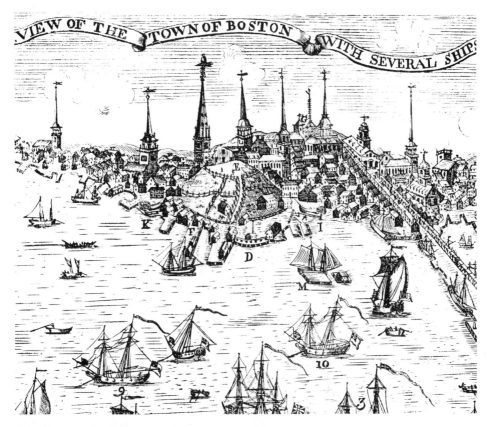

Six years after Paul Revere made an engraving of British troops landing in Boston, he produced another one showing a wider panorama of the town and harbour. Eight of the warships are still swinging to their anchors in the same positions but there are more small craft. These comprise two schooners at anchor with two yards on each mast; a fore-and-aft schooner under sail and another at anchor; there are also several two-masted boats without bowsprits. A small two-master having leg-of-mutton sails and a small mizen stepped right aft, making it a sort of three-masted schooner, appears at the top left of warship No. 6. One of the two-masters is rigged with sprits. [MAC-GREGOR COLLECTION].

existed for quite one hundred years on both sides of the Atlantic. In America it is
thought that some of the fishing ketches might have been rigged in a similar fashion
which would have been an improvement on the earlier rig of a single sail on each mast.
It is totally against tradition to imagine that a new class, called a 'scooner', suddenly
made its appearance and was at once universally adopted. When almost 125 years
later, the Aberdeen clipper schooner *Scottish Maid* was launched, many have fondly
imagined that all vessels subsequently built in Aberdeen possessed the new 'Aberdeen
Bow'. But this was far from the case. The 'scooning' of the Gloucester two-master
may have applied to a new hull-form rather than any alteration of an established rig.

It is convenient now to use the word 'schooner' here to describe vessels of this rig,
although shallops with two masts are treated in the next chapter.

But in spite of the use of this new word, the English continued to call a large decked
schooner a 'sloop' as late as about 1750 and a small open one a 'shallop'. The idio-
syncrasies of registration officials and of shipbuilders over rig nomenclature have

*A Dutch schooner and a British cutter at Curaçao in 1786. The Mariners Museum has a painting
done the year before showing an almost identical schooner at Curaçao but flying British colours. The
schooner here has a ringtail boom rigged out but she crosses no yards.* [PARKER GALLERY].

Model of HMS Sultana *made from Howard Chapelle's plans with square sails only on the foremast, although the schooner's log-book infers square topsails on both masts.* [MODEL SHIPWAYS].

greatly confused rig evolution for the modern student and possibly curtailed the acknowledgement of the introduction of new and varied types of rig.

Today we are always trying to pin names on things and historians often regret the anonymity adopted in past centuries. To find a named schooner of large size in 1736 is therefore something to note. This is the *St Ann* and it was in that year that this fine-lined Portuguese dispatch schooner reached Portsmouth, where a surveyor of the Royal Navy took off her lines. His plan was acquired by the Swedish naval architect Chapman on a visit to England and so resides in a Stockholm museum. But Howard I. Chapelle redrew the lines plan and reconstructed a sail plan from the listed spar dimensions, and these plans appear in his book *Search for Speed under Sail*. The *St Ann* was reported to have been built in America and had dimensions of 58 ft 2 in × 11 ft 10 in × 6 ft 10 in (keel rabbet to deck) and a tonnage of 36½. The gaffs are fairly short and there are three yards on the foremast. It is interesting that the topgallant yard was termed a 'pidgeon' yard. The French called the topgallant after another bird, a parrot, using the word *perroquet*.

As the trade with the West Indies was increasing, schooners were becoming larger in size and in particular the proportions of the gaff sails were altering as the gaffs were made longer. Economy in manpower was the keynote and that was why the sloop with a single big gaff sail and two or three square sails was gradually replaced by the schooner, with its smaller sail units. Schooners were also popular in the rapidly expanding fishing industry: in 1721 there were 120 of them at Marblehead averaging 50 tons; twenty years later the number had increased to 160. Owing to numerous pirates and little in the way of naval protection, schooners were often designed to sail fast to elude capture, and some were armed.

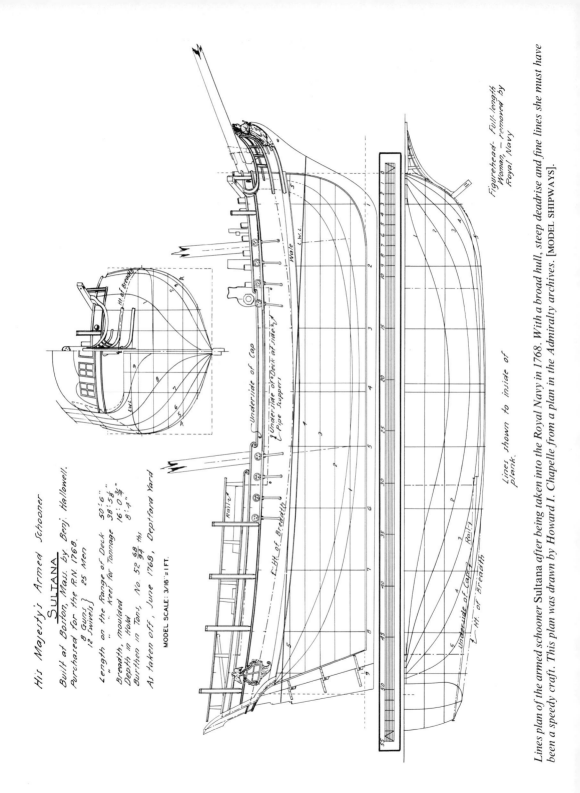

His Majesty's Armed Schooner
SULTANA

Built at Boston, Mass. by Benj. Hallowell.
Purchased for the R.N. 1768.
8 Guns }
12 Swivels } 25 Men

Length on the Range of Deck   50'6''
   ''   '' ''   Keel for Tonnage 38'5⅝''
Breadth, moulded   16'0¾''
Depth in Hold   8'4''
Burthen in Tons, No. 52 68/94 ths
As taken off, June 1768, Deptford Yard

MODEL SCALE: 3/16''=1 FT.

Figurehead- Full-length
Woman,- removed by
Royal Navy

Lines shown to inside of
plank.

Lines plan of the armed schooner Sultana after being taken into the Royal Navy in 1768. With a broad hull, steep deadrise and fine lines she must have been a speedy craft. This plan was drawn by Howard I. Chapelle from a plan in the Admiralty archives. [MODEL SHIPWAYS].

Marblehead-built schooners in the thirty or so years prior to the War of Independence gained a reputation for speed and the Royal Navy purchased six of them in the years 1767-8. One of them was the *Sultana* which was built at Boston in 1767 and bought the following year. She was of 50⅔ tons with a length on deck of 50ft 6in and a breadth of 16ft 1in. She had two yards on each mast and longish gaffs. Another schooner was the *Chaleur*, somewhat larger at 121 tons with a plain unadorned stem. She could set square topsails on both masts, as well as a square foresail. This sail arrangement was becoming very popular for the period up to 1815 on both sides of the Atlantic. Two further schooners were built in New York in 1767 especially for the Royal Navy. Plans of all these have survived in the British Admiralty records.

In *The National Watercraft Collection*, Howard Chapelle quotes from the Boston Gazette of May 1761 which warned of a 12-gun French privateer off the coast that had originally been a 'Marblehead fisherman', and now had black upperworks on one side of her hull but was painted yellow with white streaks on the other side. In 1777, the same paper warned of another Marblehead-built schooner, her bottom painted white and of about 70 tons with a crew of 40. Her rig is described as having a 'lug foresail and two standing topsails'. The topsails would be a square topsail on each mast; lug foresails were occasionally to be seen and also during the nineteenth century. The mainsail would have been a gaff sail.

A painting of the schooner *Baltick* in the Peabody Museum is constantly being reproduced. Dated 1765, it is important as probably being the earliest portrait of a named schooner. The foremast is stepped well forward, there is a high steeved bowsprit, a square topsail and also a big square foresail in addition to the gaff sail on each mast. Steering on all schooners at this time was by means of a tiller, and all these schooners had square sterns.

CHAPTER FOUR

Shallops and Chebacco Boats

Two types of schooner-rigged craft had emerged by 1750 in America: one was the ocean-going schooner used on long coastal voyages or in the deepsea fisheries, and rigged with square as well as fore-and-aft canvas; the other was a generally smaller craft used for estuary and inshore work, but noteworthy because she only carried two gaff sails of roughly similar size, without either bowsprit or jib. Of this latter category were the shallops which were decked vessels rigged with gaffsails or spritsails, and with the foremast stepped right up in the eyes of the boat.

Such craft were also in use in England and there is a most interesting painting by John Clevely of various vessels on the River Stour near Ipswich, including two shallops. What makes this picture unique is that an X-ray photograph of the shallops taken by the National Maritime Museum, which owns the painting, reveals that the rig was originally that of gaff sails on two masts with short gaffs but that it had been over-painted so as to alter the rig to two spritsails. For the most part the English shallop was a somewhat smaller vessel and was often un-decked. An engraving by Kips of the Thames at Lambeth, dated c1671, depicts just such a craft measuring about 25 feet in length. But another important difference compared with the American shallop was that the English one usually had a bowsprit from which a large jib was set.

After the end of the American War of Independence, there was a shortage of the larger schooners for the growing coastal fisheries, and so an enlargement of the shallop was developed at Essex, Massachusetts, with a tonnage of about 25 which gave an average length of 38 feet and a beam of 11½ feet. They continued to have the foremast stepped right up in the eyes without a jib, and two types of hull emerged: one was the Chebacco boat which had a cat stern; the other was the shorter and smaller 'Dogbody' with a square stern. The cat stern was developed from the pink, but the overhang of the deck was not so extreme. It was really a double-ended hull in which the wales, rather than terminating at the point where quarter piece and wing transom met, as in a square stern, continued round to the sternpost. These two types were popular until about 1815. When fishing, the men used to stand in a series of small wells, presumably to give them security as there was often no bulwark –just a low wash board.

The Chebacco boats were built in New England, New Brunswick and Nova Scotia. The now extinct Saint John River 'woodboats' were descended from them, as well as the double-ended fishing boats still to be seen around the Gaspé coast.

In England, Daniel Brocklebank built four schooner-rigged shallops between 1799 and 1806 and a sail plan of one is reproduced here. Her size was that of an average

Chebacco boat but she was probably not decked over. These four were exported to the West Indies for use in carrying hogsheads of sugar from small harbours to waiting ships which lay at anchor. The Chebacco boat usually had long gaffs, a boom for the foresail, and no bowsprit or jib. At Castletown, Isle of Man, the shallop *Peggy* of 1791 has survived. She was clinker-built and originally carried two drop keels. Small survivors of the shallops were the open-decked schooner-rigged lighters used at Padstow as late as the first decade of the present century.

Ink drawing attributed to Samuel Owen (1768-1857) of a shallop hoisting sail. Two of the crew are inked in; there is a third drawn in pencil or he may be an alternate for the one hoisting the mainsail. [MacGREGOR COLLECTION].

This early photograph taken by Calvert Jones about 1845 in Swansea Harbour shows two of the 21-foot schooner-rigged pilot boats. Nearest is S 4, named Faith *and beside the quay is S 7, the* Neptune. *They were only partially decked and each has a cockpit at the stern and around the foot of the mainmast; the bowsprits have been run in-board; the long main boom is lying along the port side; the short gaffs, less than 6 ft long, must be under the sails. Larger decked boats appeared about 1860.* [NATIONAL MARITIME MUSEUM].

About the turn of the century there were certainly two schooner-rigged barges or shallops to be seen in Padstow harbour. Cargoes of heavily-laden schooners were partly off-loaded into these barges at the mouth of the River Camel to let the larger vessels get up the river on a smaller draft. The barge was of shallow draft, flat-bottomed with two pole masts and no bowsprit. The hold filled the area between the masts.
[ROYAL CORNWALL INSTITUTION].

CHAPTER FIVE

Privateers and Baltimore Clippers

The fast-sailing Marblehead schooners were described in Chapter Three but there were two other important types. One was the 'Virginia pilot boat' with a flush deck, deep drag aft, practically no bulwarks and with primitive accommodation. They were rigged with two well-raked pole masts which carried a gaff mainsail on a boom and a gaff foresail without a boom; and there was a bowsprit which carried a large jib. Square canvas was rare but there was a large main topmast staysail. They were also popular at New York and on the Delaware and averaged 35 to 45 feet in length.

The other type was built on Chesapeake Bay and was a bigger schooner altogether, carrying square topsails and topgallants on the foremast and sometimes also on the mainmast. Like the Virginia model, there was a low profile hull with a deep drag aft; there was usually steep deadrise and fine waterlines to give maximum speed under sail. Even by 1757 some of these schooners were 80 feet long and mounted fourteen guns. This was the type which became known as a 'Baltimore clipper'. Plans of captured American vessels were made by surveyors of the Royal Navy which enable one to obtain a good idea of the splendid schooners sailing the high seas in those days and establish the fact that the design was truly American and not taken from French luggers, which is the popular legend.

Naval architecture in the principal maritime nations in Europe had developed over the years along established lines, but in the newly developed American States ship design was not only experimental but was made to suit the circumstances of the moment. Ornamentation was virtually non-existent and the stem rarely had anything more than a fiddle head under the bowsprit, which provided the latter with additional support in the form of a knee to which the gammon lashing could be secured. Below this the stem usually curved away into the keel; and aft, there was considerable rake to the sternpost. The bulwarks were only high enough to allow gun ports to be formed in them. An example of an extremely fine-lined schooner was the *Nonpareil*, built in 1801 on Chesapeake Bay, with a length on deck of 89 ft 6 in and a moulded beam of 22 ft 10 in. She was taken into the Royal Navy in 1808.

Between 1783 when the War of Independence terminated and 1812 when the Naval War began, it was found that Baltimore clippers built on extreme lines did not carry enough cargo and so the hull-form was made a little fuller. Nevertheless they were still fast by most standards. An example of this modified class was the *Fly* which was captured in 1811 and taken into the Royal Navy under the name of *Sea Lark*. She had a tonnage of 178.

Howard I. Chapelle records that the three-masted schooner first appeared on the

Chesapeake in about 1795 and was usually of the Virginia pilot boat model, and resulted in the desire to increase the sail area on a small hull. Some of these were sold to the French. Bermuda builders also copied these three-masters and in the early decades of the nineteenth century they gave them leg-of-mutton sails on each mast, thus rigging them with a Bermuda schooner rig. An oil painting by J. Lynn dated 1834 in the Macpherson Collection at the National Maritime Museum shows such a schooner with a crew of six. According to the size of the figures, she would be about 70ft long overall. The bowsprit carries one big jib; the mainmast is the tallest and the mizen rather short; the sails are hooped to the masts; she has a vertical stem and a long counter; she is flush-decked with low bulwarks; and a white ensign is flying from the mizen truck. The foresail and mainsail are boomless and the mizen projects over the stern.

In this watercolour sketch by Admiral Philip Brown, entitled 'The Midas *of Baltimore bound to Bordeaux', the schooner is drawn stern-on with the masts in line; the lower crosstrees are those on the foremast. She has a great vareity of flying kites set, and the triangular area between the sailor in the rigging and the mainmast could be the lowered peak of the fore gaff sail or else the head yard of some other fancy sail about to be set. [MACGREGOR COLLECTION].*

An unidentified schooner photographed in stereo at Havana. She is a smaller vessel than the topsail schooner on page 28, with shorter topmasts, but she does cross a short yard on the foremast. She is obviously another survivor from the past with her low-peaked main gaff and boomless foresail. [NATIONAL MARITIME MUSEUM, SAN FRANCISCO].

Two fine-lined schooners, the *Enterprise* and *Experiment*, formed units of the first American Navy in the 1790s; other fast-sailing schooners were employed as Revenue Cutters. In 1808, no less than nine of the twelve large schooners in the Royal Navy were built in America. Baltimore clippers were also rigged as true brigantines, brigs and full-rigged ships. Many of the schooners carried so much square canvas on the foremast that they virtually became brigantines in a following wind.

During the Naval War of 1812, the size of Chesapeake schooners increased to 115 ft long on deck but this was found to be about the maximum size that could be handled. The two principal sails, the foresail and mainsail, became excessively large at this size and the main boom was an unwieldy spar.

After the end of the war, brigs and brigantines were increasingly used on ocean trades and the building of sharp-bodied schooners was for sale to owners in Central

This splendid photograph taken in Havana, Cuba, in 1860 and made from a stereo plate, shows an unidentified schooner entering the harbour. Morro Castle is on the port bow. Whether she is of clipper-build cannot be determined but she looks like a survivor from the past. Worth noting is how the colour of bowsprit and main boom, projecting beyond the hull, changes from dark to light. [PEABODY MUSEUM, SALEM].

and Southern America for use as privateers, warships or carrying of illicit cargoes. Not a few were also used to carry slaves.

An account of a voyage in a Baltimore clipper was published in 1847 as one of the chapters in *Life on the Ocean*. Its author, George Little, born in 1792, had a poetic turn of phrase:

'Once more then, [in December 1825], I am in command of one of the most beautiful models of a vessel that ever floated on the ocean–I mean a Baltimore clipper schooner, of one hundred and forty tons burthen, with proportions scrupulously exact as if turned out of a mould. The workmanship was in all respects as neatly executed as if intended as a beautiful specimen of cabinet excellence; her spars were in perfect symmetry of proportions with the hull, and she sat upon the water like the seabird that sleeps at ease on the mountain billow. The destination of this beautiful craft was a hazardous one, because it was in the vicinity of those seas infested by pirates, viz. the Gulf of Mexico. Her intended employment was mainly to bring specie from thence to the United States. She was well armed and manned, and possessed a pair of heels, as report had it, that would outstrip the wind.'

The crew numbered sixteen, and on this passage she passed the Moro light on the seventh night after leaving Cape Henry, out of Baltimore. At Tampico, Campeachy and other ports, specie, indigo, cochineal and logwood were loaded for Baltimore, and the return passage was made to complete a round voyage of seven weeks. George Little made six such voyages in command, and describes a brush with a pirate:

'The schooner was at this time running under foresail alone, the other sails being lowered down, but not furled . . . The stranger rounded to under our lee . . . My men

The schooner Challenge *exhibits the limit of square canvas that could be set on a schooner. Here the yards on the main are shorter than those on the fore and the square sail from the fore yard has been clewed up.* [PEABODY MUSEUM, SALEM].

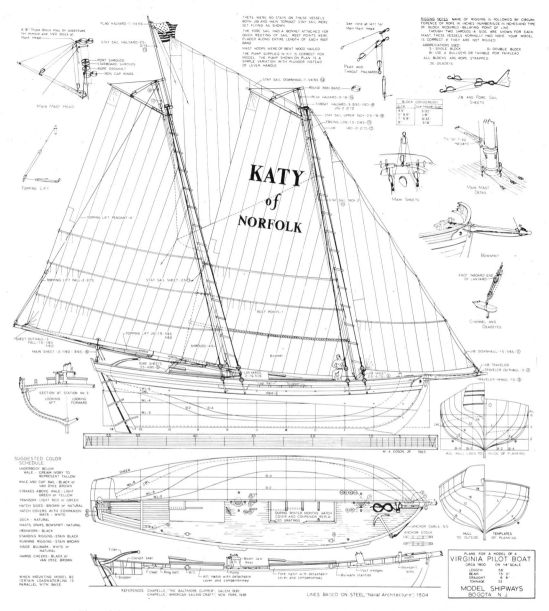

Plan of the Virginia pilot boat Katy *(c1800) with dimensions of 56 ft × 15 ft 3 in and 52 tons. Plan drawn by M. A. Edson jnr.* [MODEL SHIPWAYS].

were stationed, some at the main-halyards, others at the fore-topsail and jib-halyards.

'At length the looked-for moment came, the pirate's boat was swung in the tackles over the side, our sails went cheerily aloft, and in a few minutes our craft was bounding over the sea at the rate of ten knots per hour . . . Shot after shot passed over us, but as yet none had done any execution and as it became necessary to increase our speed, in order to get out of gun-shot if possible, orders were given to get the squaresail aloft, ease off the main-sheet, and run the long nine-pounder aft. These orders were instantly executed, and with the additional press of canvass, she, like a dolphin when hard chased by the ravenous shark, seemed to jump out of the water, for she was now running off twelve knots; . . . but as the distance between us was increasing every moment, and the pirate, no doubt becoming exasperated at our superior sailing, yawed and gave us his whole broadside, which cut away the lower studding-sail boom, and one shot passed through our squaresail. This was his last success . . . Then we returned his coaxing civilities in compliments of his own heart's choice, by letting him have a shot from our long nine-pounder.'

On his fifth voyage, after having beaten off an attack at midnight by two Spanish armed boats under oars at the mouth of Campeachy harbour, Captain Little set sail but shortly after was chased by the pirate Gibbs for a day and a night.

'Our craft was dressed with all the canvas that could be set, and hauled up so that every sail would draw on the starboard tack. The pirate was no laggard. Hour after hour passed, and no perceptible difference was discovered in the sailing of the two vessels . . .

'At meridian it could not be ascertained that either vessel had the advantage in sailing; but the wind now began to slacken its force, and as in a light breeze nothing that was ever built could probably sail faster than this beautiful craft, it became evident that she was stealing away from the pirate.' The latter then opened fire but no shots struck home and at sunset the schooner had gained a mile but continued all night 'under a heavy press of sail'.

'At daylight, in the morning, the pirate was again about a gun-shot and a half astern, under a cloud of canvas. Our studding-sails were again set, but not without the expectation of losing the booms, sails, &c. as the wind blew strong, and our craft was bounding over the sea at the rate of twelve knots. It was hard, although a most splendid chase, and I know not how it would have terminated, if we had not, at 10 o'clock, fallen in with the American man-of-war schooner *Shark*, which, when discovered by the pirate, caused him to take in sail, and haul upon a wind. The last we saw of him was in full flight from the man-of-war, although he appeared to out-sail the *Shark* with ease.'

Howard I. Chapelle in the *National Watercraft Collection* writes that the *Spark* was the fastest vessel in the American navy at the end of the 1812-15 War and for some years afterwards, so this was probably the brig which succoured George Little and his crew. Unfortunately, Little omits to give the name of the schooner he commanded.

CHAPTER SIX

British Schooners before 1835

Just as there were two classes of schooners in America in the eighteenth century – the larger sea-going variety with additional square canvas and the smaller 'shallop type' with not much more canvas than two gaff sails – so the same can be said for Great Britain. The shallops have already been described in Chapter Four, and here we can now examine the larger schooners which were also suitable for ocean-going passages.

One would like to think that the arrival of the Portuguese schooner *St Ann* caused a stir at Portsmouth in 1736, but it is impossible to tell as there is no evidence that her lines and sail plan were copied. The first schooner registered in the Royal Navy was the *Barbadoes* of 130 tons, which was built in Virginia and bought at Antigua in 1757. Then six Marblehead-built schooners were purchased in 1767-68 to protect the New England fisheries and two further schooners were actually ordered from yards in New York, namely the *Earl of Egmont* and *Sir Edward Hawke*.

The French lexicographer, Antoine Lescallier, stated in his *Vocabulaire des Termes de Marine* in 1777 that schooners were mostly used in England and America and that the sails resembled the mainsail of a brigantine or cutter. He added that there were two or three jibs, a topsail on each mast, and a square sail to be set when running before the wind. Among the principal maritime writers, Falconer in England, Chapman in Sweden and Groenewegen in Holland, each gives a single engraving of a schooner showing that the rig was known but not used much. The majority of examples also allot a square topsail and also a top-gallant when set on both fore and main masts. As in America, the gaffs had now increased in length to the proportions seen in the nineteenth century, and bowsprits and jibbooms were often excessively long. A spritsail yard may have helped to stiffen the latter but until the dolphin striker made its appearance in the last quarter of the eighteenth century there must have been many problems here.

There is a plan in the Admiralty Collection at the National Maritime Museum of the clinker-built schooner *Helena* of 245 tons, built in 1778 with a length of 76 ft 5½ in on deck and a large beam of 26 ft 9 in which gave her the proportions of a cutter. She was pierced for eighteen guns. Her main lower mast was 81 ft long. The English were adept at designing and building fast cutters in which they concentrated their skills to obtain fast-sailing hulls, and if the hull's size became too large to be adequately rigged with only one mast, then a schooner or brig's rig was given her. Hence the term 'cutter-brig'.

The American version of a fast-sailing hull was basically of a longer and narrower type and well-suited for the schooner rig. It needed a disciplined reappraisal by the

The venerable schooner Jane was built at Pwllheli in 1827 and in 1879 measured 71.0ft × 17.3ft × 10.2ft and 94 tons. She had been lengthened in 1855 and again in 1869; and so had probably begun life as a sloop or galliot with only one mast. She had a round stern and is being steered with a tiller. [BASIL LAVIS COLLECTION].

The bluff-bowed Alert, seen here at Whitby, has the hull of a collier brig and with her round stern was probably a bully boy. Of 43 tons, she was built at Whitby in 1802. The topsail yard is hanging on its lifts from the lower mast cap, which was then a common practice on the East Coast; the topgallant has been lowered below the cap, so it could not have had a mast parral. [NAUTICAL PHOTO AGENCY].

English to design a new sort of fine-lined hull which could readily be rigged as a schooner. One way, practised in the second quarter of the nineteenth century, was to cut a cutter in half, drag the halves apart and build in a new centre section of ten or fifteen feet in length. Construction of merchant schooners occurred occasionally, but with the name of *Experiment* frequently given the craft it may be inferred that the builder was not sanguine of any great success. For instance, this was the name Daniel Brocklebank gave his first schooner in 1802 and the second schooner did not appear until 1822. In fact, in 1811 he altered the schooner *Defiance* into a brig. What an indignity!

To show the lack of interest in schooner-building in England, David Steel's folio of plans published in 1805 with his *Naval Architecture* does not include a single British-built schooner, although there are plans of three American schooners and the offsets of a fourth. Some rigged models in the Science Museum, London, illustrate the sort of armed schooners serving in the Royal Navy.

One of these models has the hull of a contemporary dockyard model of about 1775 and she is pierced for a broadside of six guns on the open deck; there is a short poop

A model made by Mr F. Hinchliffe of HMS Hornet *built in 1831 at Chatham. Of 181 tons B.M. she measured 81 ft × 23 ft 6 in and carried six guns. She was broken up in 1845.* [EDWARD BOWNESS].

Pencil drawing entitled: 'J. C. 1820. HM Schooner Augusta. *Tender to HMS* Amphion *off Bus. Ay.'. Presumably off Buenos Ayres. The leech of the foresail is visible because the mainsail tack has been hauled up; the gaffs are fairly short; there is a topmast stunsail set abaft the fore topsail; but two shrouds on the foremast and only one on the main suggest a small craft.* [MAC GREGOR COLLECTION].

and fo'c'sle; a capstan abaft the mainmast but no windlass. The spars were made in 1902 when she was rigged, and show square sails on the foremast only. Another is of the *Express* and was made from the original draught and rigged with the aid of the spar dimensions listed. Built at Portsmouth in 1815, her hull looks to be strongly influenced by the Virginian pilot boat model.

Another experimentation with the schooner rig occurred with a sloop designed by the Admiralty in 1802 for use at Port Jackson–now named Sydney. But in the following year she was altered to a schooner. I reconstructed her probable rig from proportions given by the naval architect John Fincham and published her plan in *Merchant Sailing Ships 1775-1815*. The schooner was 53ft long on deck and 17ft 6in beam.

The close connection with a cutter that existed in the British Isles in the matter of speed was responsible in giving schooners plain vertical stems with the bowsprit set to port or starboard of the stem head and with almost no steeve. There are spar dimensions for the schooner *Plough* which Alexander Hall built at Aberdeen in 1811 of 86 tons for owners at Newburgh. She was 60½ft length for tonnage and 18ft 8in breadth and cost £10 per ton. She had topsails and topgallants on each mast and the lengths of fore gaff and boom had to be determined by the builder, as the specification reads: 'Fore boom and gaff to fit between the masts'. The main lower yard is called a 'crossjack yard'.

A fore-and-aft schooner drawn by Edward Gwyn c1780. The topsail masts were nothing much more than flag poles and have no trestle trees or caps. Perhaps she was intended as a yacht as there is decoration on the stern and abaft the mainmast. [NATIONAL MARITIME MUSEUM].

The deep hulls of the brig Mary *of St Ives and the schooner* Liberty *of Teignmouth at Swansea about 1845. British coasters had to have flat bottoms so as to stay upright at low tide conditions like this.* [NATIONAL MARITIME MUSEUM].

Some artists pictured schooners setting topsails on each mast but a square top-gallant on the foremast only, as in the case of the American schooner *Fame* of Salem, built in 1795; but just occasionally there are square sails on the mainmast only and none on the fore as in J. F. W. Des Barres illustration from *The Atlantic Neptune* dated 1779, as reproduced in *Sailing Ships of the Maritimes* by Dr Charles A. Armour.

Apart from three-masted schooners built in America or Bermuda, a few were constructed in Great Britain such as the *Jenny* and *Curlew*, both sailing in the 1790s. At Lancaster in 1807, John Brockbank contracted to build a schooner of 153 tons with three masts at a cost of £10. 10s. per ton. The amount of square canvas in any of these is not known.

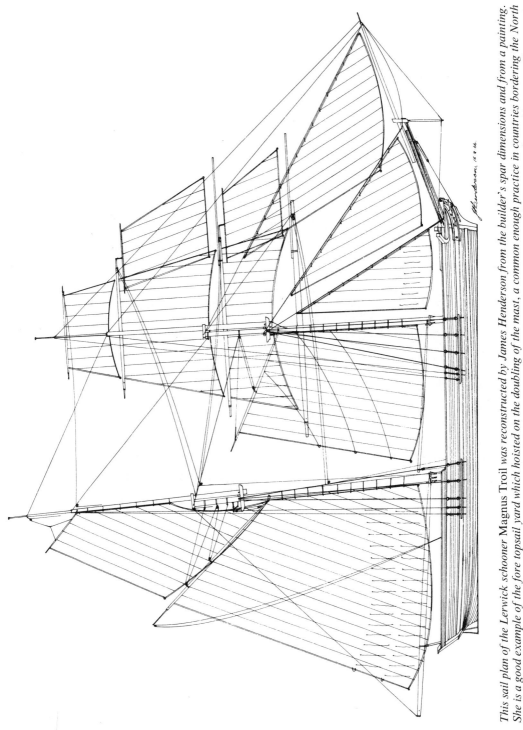

This sail plan of the Lerwick schooner Magnus Troil was reconstructed by James Henderson from the builder's spar dimensions and from a painting. She is a good example of the fore topsail yard which hoisted on the doubling of the mast, a common enough practice in countries bordering the North Sea. She sets a topgallant and royal too. She was built at Aberdeen in 1830 by Alexander Hall & Sons of 124 tons and cost £9 per ton. Her name is from a character in one of Sir Walter Scott's novels. [JAMES HENDERSON].

CHAPTER SEVEN

Schooner–Brigantines

If a two-masted schooner carries lower, topsail, topgallant and royal yards on the foremast and if the mast is in two pieces with a lower mast and fidded topmast, she is fully acceptable to class as a 'schooner'. (By the way, there would, of course, be a gaff sail on both the fore and main lower masts, and the mainsail would be set on a boom even if the foresail was not.) But if that part of the foremast on which the top-gallant and royal yards are crossed be a separately fidded mast–in fact, a topgallant mast–and if all the gaff sails remain as before, is she then still a schooner?

This three-piece mast is what the purists call a 'square-rigged' mast. But if the fore and main lower masts are of approximately equal height and no fore course is

This watercolour by Charles Shlei done at Riga in 1831, depicts the Hero *of Dundee under full sail. It is an interesting rig combination: the foremast is a three-piece mast with a proper fore top; the royal mast is fidded abaft the topgallant mast; there is a bentinck boom to the foresail; the fore gaff sail or perhaps, more properly, the fore trysail, as it hoists on a trysail mast, is set on a boom. But she is more a 'brigantine-schooner' than the other way round. The scale in feet below the title is unusual.* [ALTONAER MUSEUM, HAMBURG].

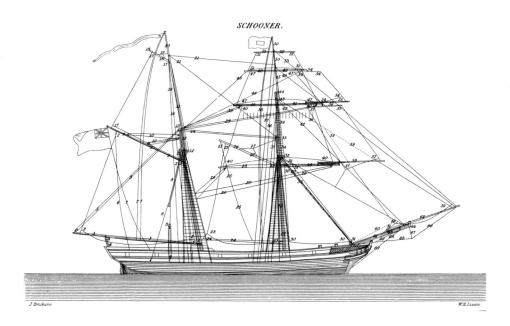

SCHOONER.

J.Brisbane   W.H.Lizars

NUMERICAL INDEX TO SCHOONER.

1 MAIN MAST.
2 Main Sail.
3 Main Boom.
4 Main Sheet (and M. S. Block).
5 Main Boom Topping Lift.
6 Vangs of Main Gaff.
7 Signal Halyards.
8 Runner and Tackle.
9 Main Gaff.
10 Main Peak Halyards.
11 Main Throat Halyards.
12 Main Cross-trees.
13 Main Cap.
14 Main Stay.
15 *Main Topmast*.
16 Maintopmast Backstays.
17 Gaff Topsail.
18 Gaff Topsail Gaff.
19 Gaff Topsail Halyards.
20 Pole of Main Topmast.
21 Maintopmast Stay.
22 FORE MAST.
23 Fore Spencer.
24 Fore Spencer Boom.

25 Fore Spencer Vangs.
26 Fore Spencer Gaff.
27 Fore Peak Halyards (connected to Gaff by the *bridle*).
28 Fore Yard.
29 Fore Braces.
30 Fore Sail and Fore Stay.
31 Fore Staysail (and Halyards.)
32 Fore Cross-trees.
33 Fore Cap.
34 *Foretopmast*.
35 Foretopmast Backstays.
36 Foretopgallant Backstays.
37 Fore Royal Backstay.
38 Signal Halyards.
39 Foretopsail Braces.
40 Foretopsail.
41 Foretopsail Yard.
42 Foretopmast Stay.
43 Foretopmast Cross-trees.
44 Foretopmast Cap.
45 Foretopgallant Mast.
46 Foretopgallant Braces.
47 Foretopgallant Sail.

48 Foretopgallant Yard.
49 Foretopgallant Stay.
50 *Fore Royal Mast* and *Pole*.
51 Fore Royal.
52 Fore Royal Yard.
53 Fore Royal Stay.
54 Foretopgallant Studding Sail and Yard.
55 Foretopgallant Studding Sail Boom.
56 Foretopmast Studding Sail Yard.
57 Foretopmast Studding Sail.
58 Foretopmast Studding Sail Boom.
59 Jib, and Jib Stay.
60 Jib Sheet.
61 Bowsprit.
62 Bowsprit Shrouds.
63 Bowsprit Heart.
64 Bowsprit Cap.
65 Jib Boom.
66 Martingale Stay.
67 Martingale.
68 Martingale Back-ropes.
69 Bobstay.

Key and sail plan to illustrate 'Schooner' in Arthur Young's Nautical Dictionary, *published at Dundee in 1846. He terms the foresail a 'fore spencer'.* [MacGREGOR COLLECTION].

bent on the fore yard, is the three-piece foremast really a properly square-rigged mast? Should she be called a brigantine or a schooner?

It is this very rig variation which is used by Arthur Young to illustrate his definition of the word 'Schooner' in his *Nautical Dictionary*, first published at Dundee in 1846. See illustration above.

Returning to the case of the schooner with a three-piece foremast, northern Europeans had a useful name for this sort of rig which they called '*schunerbrigg*' or 'schoonerbrig'. They also embraced under this category what we in Britain should call a 'brigantine'. Perhaps our terminology should be 'schooner-brigantine' but whatever the name it makes a very attractive rig. There is a good balance between square and fore-and-aft canvas: the vessel must have been able to point up into the wind as well as a schooner, but with a fair wind on the quarter or from astern she had a complete mast of square canvas that was augmented by stunsails on each side. In his *Treatise on Masting Ships* (2nd edition 1843), John Fincham has a table for two-masted vessels termed 'brig forward and schooner aft' which produces a rig that is roughly equivalent to the European term.

The schooner-brigantine was popular from the 1820's for about sixty years or so but especially in the first half of the century. In Britain and North Europe, hulls were still heavy without much deadrise and cargo-carrying was all important. For voyages to get fresh fruit from the Azores or dried fruit from the Mediterranean, a faster craft was needed to prevent deterioration of the cargo, and also to avoid seizure by pirates. A long nine-pounder gun on a pivot was a regular armament, as well as muskets and pikes for the crew. The large sail area was effectual in making fast passages and consequently the rig was popular amongst opium clippers.

The 'schooner packet' *St Helena*, built in 1814 for the Honourable East India Company, was an early example of a schooner-brigantine. She was employed to

Sail plan and longitudinal section of the St. Helena *showing the two lower masts of equal height and a fidded fore topgallant. She was built on the Thames in 1814. Reconstructed by David R. MacGregor.* [AUTHOR].

take supplies to the Island in the South Atlantic after which she was named, and a lines plan reproduced in *Fast Sailing Ships* shows her to have the hull-form of a brig with a length of 81 ft 3 in on deck and a beam of 20 ft 7 in which gave a tonnage of 135. She cost £21 per ton to build at the Blackwall Yard on the River Thames. Her first tour of duty lasted until 1821 and she was crewed by a master, two mates, a bosun, carpenter, eight seamen and one landsman. The seamen were paid £2.50 per month, bosun and 'chips' got £5 each, and the master £30. Her log-book tells of many repairs carried out on board including the making of new spars and sails. Off St Helena she had to refit at sea, and in order to careen her to repair her copper sheathing, she was stripped of all her spars and rigging down to her lower masts, and it was all sent ashore.

In 1819 on 2nd August she was struck by a severe squall, bound to Cape Town from St Helena during which she 'carried away fore and main topmasts, flying jibbom and fore top-g-mast, split the gaff foresail, main topmast staysail and top-g-sail'. Two days after the loss of the topmasts new ones had been made, probably from half-completed spars carried on deck, which were then fidded to allow the topsails to be set again. Seamen were well-capable of these tasks in those days but the carpenter was logged as being 'sick from frequent intoxication'. On this trip she returned to the Island in 12 days, making four consecutive day runs of 158, 172, 180 and 139 miles.

Some of the Baltimore clippers such as the *Prince de Neuchâtel* were almost

The Frankfort Packet *carried four yards on her foremast and with her square sail set from the lower yard was much like a brigantine. The topsail hoists on the doubling and so is not so deep as the topgallant. She was built at Leith in 1818 of 127 tons and this portrait was painted by F. Albinus of Hamburg.* [PARKER GALLERY].

Some vessels like the Lizzie Garrow *did not have a fidded topgallant mast but at the hounds of the long topmast, crosstrees were fitted with appropriate rigging to stiffen the mast. Built by William Date at Kingsbridge in 1854 with a length of 92.6 ft and tonnages of 218 o.m. and 174 n.m., she traded to the Mediterranean and the West Indies; she was rigged as a brig by 1860.* [FAIRWEATHER COLLECTION].

schooner-brigantines with a large gaff foresail. Similarly rigged, but without the tiny square main topgallant carried by the latter, the fruit schooner *Hellas* of 1832 was termed a 'schooner' in her day. Later she became an opium clipper.

A few schooners were built in the nineteenth century with four yards on each mast. A print of the *Amy Stockdale* off Dover was published in 1839 depicting her under sail with a big gaff mainsail and an equally large boomless gaff foresail set, two head-sails, and a square topsail–probably reefed–on each mast. The topgallants on each mast were clewed up and the royal yards were not crossed. Although no squaresail is bent on the foreyard, one was undoubtedly available in fair winds. She could really be called a 'schooner brig'. Another of this type was the *Dorothea* of 182 tons, built at Nordby, Denmark, in 1869-70. According to a photograph in *Fanø-Sejlskibe* by Frode Holm-Petersen she resembled *Amy Stockdale* but carried staysails from the mainmast instead of a gaff sail on the fore.

Alexander Hall of Aberdeen had built the schooner *Plough* in 1812 with topsails and topgallants on each mast. His next schooner was the *James* of Portsoy, built in 1821, and also with two square sails on each mast, but she was the last so built at his yard. The *Matilda* of 1829 which cost £8. 12s. 6d. per ton to build was termed in the contract to be a 'schooner or hermaphrodite'.

Other examples from south-west England and elsewhere show that the sort of rig described in this chapter was sometimes carried on a three-piece and sometimes on a two-piece mast and that the permutations were too great to be covered by a hard-and-fast definition.

CHAPTER EIGHT

Clipper Schooners

The evolution and development of the sharp-bodied fast-sailing English cutter is now well established as a precursor of the clipper, but even when the cutter's rig of a single mast with its enormous gaff sail, numerous headsails, additional square canvas and an assortment of flying kites is replaced with the two masts of schooner or brig, nothing more has been achieved than a rig variation on an immense cutter's hull. At what stage did the new concept of a schooner dawn on English minds? The cutter's proportion of beams to length was 3:1 or sometimes even less, which resulted in a very broad hull but one that possessed great power to carry sail.

The broad, short proportions of the cutter were influenced by an act of Parliament

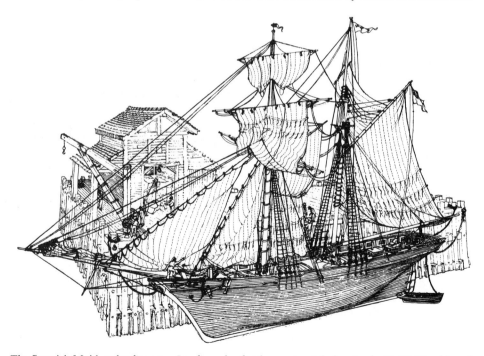

The Scottish Maid *unloading at a London wharf at low water. Ink drawing by T. W. Ward based on plans drawn by the Author.* [AUTHOR].

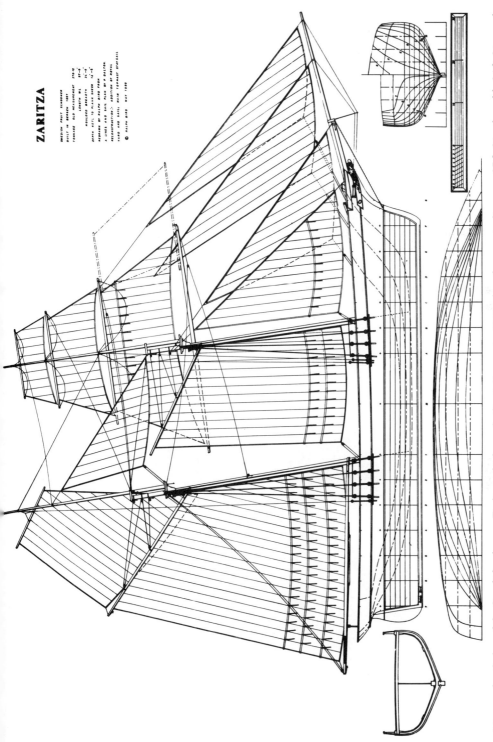

ZARITZA

SWEDISH FRUIT SCHOONER
BUILT IN BERGEN, 1857
TONNAGE OLD MEASUREMENT   270 O
                LENGTH W.L. 97-9
         MOULDED BREADTH   24-9
DEPTH KEEL TO PLANK SHEER   13-6

REDRAWN BY RALPH BIRD FROM
A LINES AND SAIL PLAN BY P DALTON
RECONSTRUCTION: ADDITION OF HULL
YARD AND SAIL MAIN TOPMAST STAYSAIL
© RALPH BIRD   MAY 1988

Lines and sail plan of the Swedish schooner Zaritza which was built at Bergen in 1857: length on waterline was 97ft 9in, breadth 24ft 9in, and tonnage 270 o.m. A comparatively shallow draft vessel, her large beam made her stiff enough to carry this large sail area. After the ice melted in the Baltic, she used to race fresh fruit to Sweden. This plan was reconstructed by Ralph Bird from an old plan owned by Percy Dalton. [RALPH BIRD].

in 1784 which specified a maximum beams-to-length ratio of $3\frac{1}{2}$:1 and which was still law in 1833. Its intention was to curb the smuggling habit for which some long fast luggers were being built; additionally, square-rig was acknowledged in the Act whereas fore-and-aft was suspect, except in the case of sloops.

Schooners were thus greatly influenced by the cutter's hull-form which was basically lengthened without increasing the breadth. The Bristol yard of J. M. Hilhouse built or designed six schooners in the ten years after 1815, and one of these was the 'very fast sailing schooner' *Sappho* of 1821 with a length of 83 ft 6 in. She had big deadrise with mostly convex lines and the plain cutter profile was retained as well as the drag aft. Even in 1839, the clipper brig *Anonyma* which was built as a yacht was identifiable as stemming from a cutter model. American clipper schooners may have been seen and studied by English shipbuilders but what they thought of them we cannot tell today. Usually a builder was convinced he could excel, with his own design and the skill of his own shipwrights, the vessel he was observing, even though he might make notes about her in his private journal.

Another type of schooner was developed from the brig by merely altering the rig whereby gaff sails were substituted for the square courses and the lower masts were increased in length. The schooner-brigantine *St Helena*, illustrated in chapter 7, is an example of this, and a schooner rig on the hull of a fine-lined brig was not illogical. There had to be a sufficient demand in Great Britain for fast-sailing schooners before any new developments occurred. In the 1830's the expansion of the opium trade between India and China and along the latter's coast, the growing

Photographed crossing the Bay of Biscay about 1900 under the name of Gravesend, *this schooner was built as the* Spring *by Date at Kingsbridge in 1867 for the Mediterranean fruit trade. Of 138 tons with a length of 89 ft she is here running before a quartering wind with an old single topsail set and also a main gaff topsail; only one headsail is set.* [NAUTICAL PHOTO AGENCY].

This oil painting is inscribed: 'Water Lily *off Chusan Islands 1859. T. H. Sloggett, Commander.' The schooner is a fine lofty vessel with stunsail booms on both the topsail and lower yards. She has not been identified, and no suitable vessel appears in* Lloyd's Register. *If she was an opium clipper, anonymity was part of her rig.* [PARKER GALLERY].

enthusiasm for yachting, the increasing fondness for fresh oranges and lemons, and the desire for faster conveyance in the coastal packets, all encouraged the designing and building of fast-sailing vessels for which the schooner rig was found eminently suitable.

Some fine-lined slavers were captured in these years and one, the *Theresa Secunda* was taken in 1832 when under the Spanish flag and was sold to become a yacht under the ownership of the Hon. R. F. Greville. She had a long shallow hull, big deadrise and sharp convex waterlines with dimensions of 90 ft 8 in × 21 ft 11 in × 9 ft 6 in and 177 tons. Although the foremast was only two feet shorter than the mainmast, she had a fidded topgallant mast and crossed three yards on the foremast, making her a schooner-brigantine. Hulls such as this could have inspired copies or improvements. Several yachts or fruiters were bought for the opium trade and others were specially built. The need to beat up the China Sea against the monsoon was paramount in the design, but powerful ships were required to withstand gales and typhoons, and well-armed ones to protect themselves against the many pirates.

Masters of the opium clippers were highly paid . When in temporary command of Jardine Matheson's 175-ton schooner *Mazeppa* in 1852, Alick J. Ryrie was getting

The schooner Fanny, *pictured here entering the Bay of Naples in October 1868, had been built at Kingsbridge in 1850 for Hurrell of Salcombe, presumably as a two-master, but had been lengthened in 1863 by 20ft to 95ft, at which time a mizen was probably added. Voyages had taken her to St. Michaels, Newfoundland and Bermuda.* [FAIRWEATHER COLLECTION].

£50 per month. A year later, when he got command of the brig *Audax*, his brother Phineas wrote home to their sister in Liverpool: 'As captain of a clipper he is a big swell, quite a Prince compared with the skipper of one of the ordinary description of merchant vessels.'

A vivid description of the opium clipper *Eamont* was written by Lindsay Anderson, third officer, and published under the title *A Cruise in an Opium Clipper*. She was built at Cowes by White in 1852 of 120 tons with a length of 87ft and a beam of 20ft. She was armed with four 18-pounders and two pivot guns and had a crew of about forty. Needless to say, the size of everything had increased considerably in Anderson's memory and he allots the mainboom a length 23ft longer than the schooner herself. But it was obviously long and undoubtedly 'a swinger and needed some handling'. The sail set from the fore yard is a 'balloon-squaresail'; the gaff foresail was called a 'fore trysail'. There is a good story of sailing through the surf into the harbour of Taku in Formosa and bumping across the reef in the process.

J. & R. White were notable builders of cutters and schooners at Cowes, and some idea of the continued influence of the cutter hull-form on design appears in this piece written in 1851 by Thomas White jnr in a book on shipbuilding: 'We find that the exact midship section of the *Harriet* cutter yacht, built some twenty years since for the Marquis Donegal, then Lord Belfast, was extended and adopted in the *Waterwitch* brig, of 330 tons; and the same has been carried out in the *Daring*, of 450 tons, or sufficiently so for the illustration of this point.'

Another type of clipper schooner had been produced in Aberdeen commencing with the launch in 1839 of the *Scottish Maid* of 142 tons n.m. which was built in order to compete with the packets of the Aberdeen & London Steam Navigation Co. A fast schooner was therefore required and during her construction her builders, Alexander Hall & Co., altered the shape of the bow by raking the planking rabbet right forward to follow the cutwater. The entrance was now much sharper, the knees and headrails were dispensed with and the appearance was more streamlined. The green-painted schooner cost £1700 and proved fast under sail, sometimes sailing between Aberdeen and London in forty-nine hours. The shape of her hull also resulted in reducing the register tonnage figure owing to the curious way tonnage was

A watercolour of an unknown schooner captured off Havana, Cuba, on 26 July 1858 by HMS Lapwing *with 500 slaves aboard. The artist was Capt. Montague Reilly RN who wrote the above details on the painting, adding that the schooner was built of mahogany. Each mast is a pole.* [MAC-GREGOR COLLECTION].

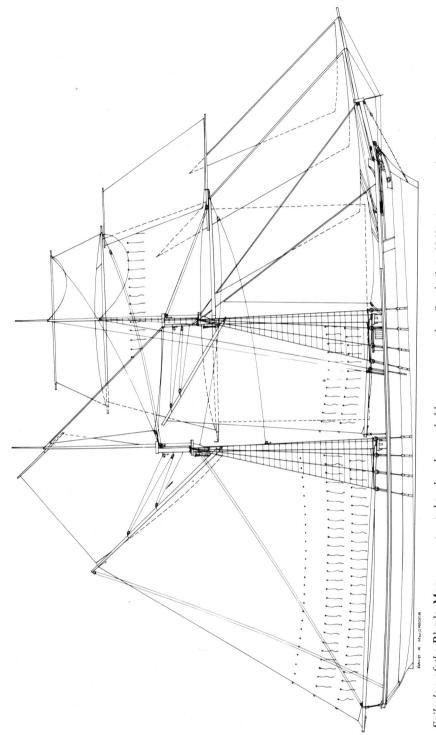

Sail plan of the Rhoda Mary reconstructed to show her probable appearance when first built in 1868. Assuming that the main topmast was not shortened when a mizen was added in 1898, the fore topmast has been increased to a comparable height. This allows a single topsail to be set and also a topgallent sail, both of which were standard when she was built. Topmast stunsails would have been carried; perhaps even topgallent and lower ones, depending on the captain's fancy. [AUTHOR].

DAVID R. MacGREGOR

then measured, thus saving port dues. Out of thirty-six vessels with the new bow – the 'Aberdeen bow' it has been called – built by Hall prior to 1848, twenty-seven of them were schooners. They certainly had an influence on the design of clipper schooners.

Shipbuilders at Dartmouth, Salcombe, Brixham, Shoreham and Ipswich as well as other ports, specialized in clipper schooners for the fresh and dried fruit trade which was at its peak in the period 1840-1870. Speed was all-important, and the sort of voyage time hoped for was the seventeen days which the schooner *Elinor* took in 1869 from London Bridge to St Michaels in the Azores and back home again.

In his celebrated handbook entitled *On The Stowage of Ships and Their Cargoes*, R. W. Stevens wrote in the 1869 edition under the section on 'Fruit':

'Several schooners belonging to Brixham are built purposely for the Mediterranean trade, and are engaged almost entirely in it; they are long flat vessels with sharp ends, but much sharper aft than forward, so much so that little or no dunnage is required beyond the ballast, which is all placed in the narrow part of the hold. One of these schooners, the *Ocean Bride*, registers 144 ton, is 120 ft overall; keel 92 ft; extreme beam 20 ft; and depth of hold 11 ft 6 in. She took in at Patras, in 1860, 180 ton (net) currants. The ballast, 20 ton, was all stowed abaft the main hatchway . . . She will stow 50 ton of St Michael's oranges – 20 boxes to the ton – with 55 ton ballast.'

The *Ocean Bride* cited here was built at Brixham by Richardson in 1859 and was owned in the same port by Sheers & Co.

The above quotation covers the chief design and stowage particulars of a typical clipper schooner of Devon or Cornwall. The reference to a 'flat vessel' probably means lack of sheer as exemplified in the lines plan of the schooner *Rhoda Mary* whose lines I drew out. This schooner was launched in 1868 in Restronguet Creek, off the western shores of the Truro River, and a paragraph in the Truro newspaper *West Britain*, commenting on her launch, reported that she was 'intended for the Baltic trade'. But she is best known as one of the three fastest schooners in the home trade, the others being the *Trevellas* and *Katie Cluet*. The sail plan I drew of her was as a three-master but she began life with two masts and so I have attempted a new reconstruction to show what she might have looked like when new.

Some three-masted schooners made their appearance in the 1850's: Gourlay Brothers of Dundee built the narrow iron-hulled *Alma* in 1854 to sail to the Australian gold fields; James Balley of Shoreham launched the *Wild Dayrell* in 1856 of 310 tons, without any square sails and with a 'Yankee three mast schooner rig' of which great things were expected; the same year, Balley built the *Osprey* with four yards on her foremast in the conventional style. *Wild Dayrell* was possibly an attempt at copying an American 'tern' schooner which was a new style. Due to the fact that so many harbours dried out at low water, British sharp-lined schooners could not afford to have deadrise or else they were in danger of falling over on their sides as the tide ebbed. The design and construction of fine-lined schooners continued throughout the nineteenth century as there were always reasons why an owner wanted a fast vessel as related in Chapter Ten.

One fast deep-sea schooner was the *Susan Vittery* which was built at Dartmouth in 1859 by W. Kelly, and after trading to the Azores and then carrying cod from Newfoundland she had the distinction of being the last schooner in the home trade to sail without an engine. Given a third mast in 1903 and renamed *Brooklands* she survived the Second World War and was finally lost near the Tuskar in 1953 when sailing under her original name.

CHAPTER NINE

North American Schooners

Writing in 1882, Henry Hall reviewed the progress of the schooner in his *Report on the Ship-Building Industry of the United States.*

'Brigs, barks, and ships were much in favor, but after 1840 they went out of use for coasters, their places being taken on the one hand by steamboats, which were built for the passenger and mail service between all the large Atlantic and Gulf ports, and on the other hand by two- and three-masted schooners, built for freighting. The fore-and-aft rig came to be preferred for coasting vessels for several reasons. Fewer sailors were required to handle the vessel, and a schooner could be worked into and out of harbors and rivers more easily than any square-rigged craft. Her trips could also, as a rule, be made in quicker time, as she could sail closer into the wind, and it was hardly necessary for her to sail from Maine to New York by way of the Bermudas, as some square-rigged vessels have done during baffling winds. The schooner rig became universal in the coasting trade about 1860, and there is probably not a bark or a ship left in this trade anywhere except on the Pacific coast, where the voyages are long and the winds blow in trades, and even there are few purely square-rigged vessels in the trade. On the lakes the schooner is the popular rig, a few square topsails being sometimes added on the forward mast.

'Originally registering no more than 40 or 50 tons, the schooner has become in course of time a large vessel, the two-masters ranging from 100 to 250 tons, the three-masters from 500 to 750 tons. The popular size now for a three-master coasting schooner on the Atlantic is about 550 or 600 tons . . .

'For transoceanic trade, and on the Pacific coast, where the waters are deep, the schooners are keel vessels with some dead rise; but on the Atlantic coast, where the harbors are so frequently shallow and obstructed with sand bars, the schooners are center-board vessels with flat bottoms. In all cases, however, the models are full, the beam large, the bow sharp and long, the run clean, and the sheer considerable forward. Above the water an American schooner has the jaunty air of a yacht. Schooners with sharp bottoms do not pay, and few are built.'

In the New England coasting business, fore-and-aft schooners of 50 to 75 feet in length were preferred from about 1825, but topsail schooners and brigantines continued to be liked for trade to the West Indies or for taking cotton from the southern ports to New York. The biggest two-master in this trade was probably the *Langdon Gilmore* of 497 old tons built in 1856 at Belleville, New Jersey. The coasting trade was by law confined to American vessels only and so was highly protected with little chance of outside influences. The smaller two-masters often set no gaff topsail on

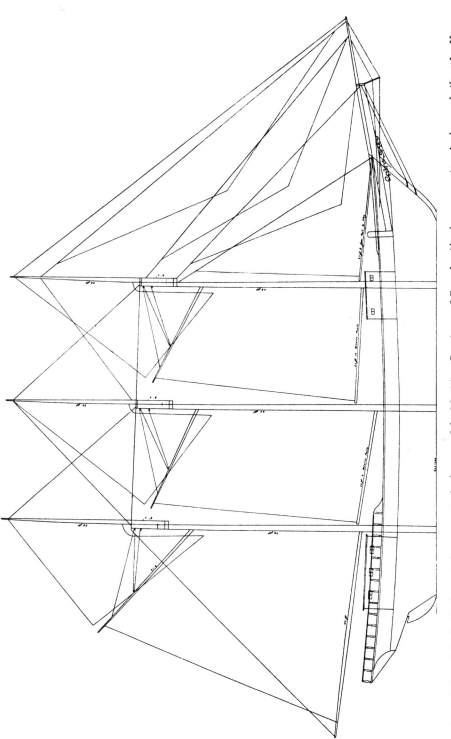

This sail plan of the A. V. Conrad shows a typical schooner of the Maritime Provinces of Canada. Also known as a 'tern', she was built at La Have, Nova Scotia, in 1908 with dimensions of 101.6ft × 27.2ft × 10.0ft and 147 tons. The height of the mainmast from deck to truck was 91 feet. This plan was traced by Dr. Charles A. Armour from the original and is reproduced through the courtesy of Everett Lohnes. [CHARLES A. ARMOUR].

This portrait of the May *shows the sort of vessel used as a packet between Boston and New York or New Orleans in the 1830s. The mizen stepped so far aft suggests that she might have been intended for a two-master. The foot of the square sail bent from the fore yard is extended on a passaree boom. Of 126 tons, she was built in 1833 at Essex, Massachusetts.* [PEABODY MUSEUM, SALEM].

the foremast and so a fore topmast was not required; of the two headsails, one hoisted on a stay to the bowsprit cap, the other went to the end of the jibboom. The main gaff topsail was hooped to the mast.

Three-masted schooners were not built much outside the Chesapeake area until the 1850s, but in that decade they suddenly became popular and forty-four of 300 tons and upwards were constructed. In this same decade, the three-masters which had all their masts of equal height without any square canvas were known as 'tern schooners' or 'terns', the word meaning three of a kind. The gaff sail on the mizen was often larger than that on the other two masts. These schooners had the simplest of rigging and needed a smaller crew than those with square canvas. Some were shallow draft with centreboards; others were much deeper like a fore-and-aft rigged Downeaster; but the most satisfactory ones were a compromise between the two, including the centreboard. Larger schooners became necessary as the shift to bulk cargoes took place in coasters after 1850, and this sort of craft became very profitable in the coal and lumber business and remained so until the end of the First World War.

Captain R. B. Forbes who introduced double topsails to America, no doubt based on the kind already employed in smaller vessels in northern Europe, also designed a form of staysail schooner which was employed successfully in 1854 on the *R. I. Evans*, which made six voyages thus rigged to the West Indies. The lower four-sided staysails were set on booms; the upper four-sided ones on a stay from the topmast; jib-headed topsails were set on booms equivalent to the conventional gaffs.

The first four-master was built on the East Coast in 1880 and was christened *William L. White* at Goss, Sawyer & Packard's yard at Bath, Maine. The rig was copied immediately and quickly became popular for vessels of 180 ft to 240 ft long.

Although it is the huge five and six-masters which have captured the imagination it should be remembered that the coastal waters were thronged with small two and three-masters of all kinds. With a skipper and a crew of only two or three, expenses were kept low and sailing close to the land ensured fresh food and an ability to keep in touch with home. One of the principal differences with British schooners was the big after deckhouse which was almost the full width of the schooner allowing a narrow passage-way each side on a level with the poop. British schooners had the after accommodation situated below decks entered through a companionway and down steep stairs, thus occupying valuable cargo space. Originally the crew of an American schooner berthed in a fo'c'sle below deck, forward, as in British vessels, but in the mid-1870s better accommodation was often demanded, especially in schooners trading with the West Indies, and this resulted in a fo'c'sle and galley being

The old schooner Polly *of Rockland was built in 1805 at Amesbury, Massachusetts, as a sloop but was re-rigged as a schooner in 1861. This photograph by Stebbins was taken in 1918. There is a cap on the bowsprit end to permit a jiboom to be fidded. The absence of a fore topmast was common practice on many American schooners.* [PEABODY MUSEUM, SALEM].

placed in a house built on the deck close abaft the foremast. In small vessels the after deckhouse was often built larger to house the crew as there was insufficient deck space for two houses.

The two-masted schooner *Mary Baker* of 101 tons, built in 1869 at Kingston, Massachusetts, sailed for many years out of Boston and New York to the West Indies, but sometimes went fishing on the Banks. Some of the Kingston fishing schooners were painted green both on deck and outside, but the *Mary Baker* had a black hull and a white strake above the waterway and a green bottom; bulwarks and deckhouse were white with blue mouldings and deck fittings were blue. Although the bowsprit was painted black, the jibboom, masts, gaffs and booms were varnished with white ends and doublings.

Howard I. Chapelle published the lines and sail plan of the three-masted schooner *Marion F. Sprague* in *History of American Sailing Ships*, describing her as 'an excellent

Built at San Francisco in 1865-66, the Dreadnought *was a scow schooner of 38 tons net and was still afloat in 1913. She would be flat-bottomed and built to carry the maximum amount of cargo. One of the crew at the foot of the mainmast is hoisting up the peak of the mainsail.* [NATIONAL MARITIME MUSEUM, SAN FRANCISCO].

Photographed under a press of sail, Bill the Butcher *was built at San Francisco in 1871 of 80 tons net*. [PEABODY MUSEUM].

example of [the] fine centerboard three-masted schooners of her period'. She was built in 1889 at East Boston, of 748 tons, having a length of 172 ft 6 in and a beam of 34 ft 3 in. She had a flat bottom, hard bilges, almost vertical sides, convex entrance, long concave run and considerable sheer. There was a raised quarter-deck which began between the fore and main masts and instead of solid bulwarks there were turned wooden balusters with a rail cap. The caps of the lower masts were level and were joined by a triatic or 'jumper' stay. To enable the small crews to hoist the large

On the Californian coast, about 100 miles nort of San Francisco, is the Albion River and Alexander Findlay describes it in his Directory for the . . . North Pacific Ocean *as being 'a very small stream, with the barest apology for a harbour at its mouth. A saw-mill upon this stream induces coasters to obtain freights here, but a great many of those trading have been lost.' It is in this situation that the schooner* Beulah *has been photographed loading timber, some of which has already been piled on her deck. A two-masted schooner with a big deck cargo lies ahead of her, ready to sail. The* Beulah *was built at San Francisco in 1882 of 339 tons net and in 1913 had a crew of seven.* [NATIONAL MARITIME MUSEUM, SAN FRANCISCO].

sails, a steam donkey boiler had been installed in all big schooners to operate winches and capstans.

Concerning competition between sail and steam, Henry Hall reported one shipbuilder at Camden, Maine, as saying in 1882: 'A three-masted schooner of 600 tons will pay better for the amount invested than a steamer in the coal business. No one would think of carrying pitch-pine on a steamer.'

The first three-master recorded as built in Canada was the *Dispatch* in 1814 on Prince Edward Island, and several were built in later decades. The first tern schooner was the *Zebra* of 142 tons, built at La Have, Nova Scotia, in 1859. There were various booms in building them and they enjoyed renewed popularity after the demise of the deepwater square rigger. This was especially true during the first two decades of the twentieth century.

The two-masted schooner on the Atlantic coast continued to be built as late as 1914 and remained in use on the Maine coast, in Chesapeake Bay and the Gulf of

In Lloyd's shipyard at Salisbury, Maryland, the three-masted schooner Hattie E. Giles *(1874 of 135 tons) has had the planking stripped from the counter timbers. The turned bulwark balusters and the davits for the stern boat are clearly shown. On the left is the two-master* Robin Hood *(1868 of 99 tons.* [MARINERS MUSEUM].

San Francisco in November or December 1864 from Steamboat Point looking along South Beach. In the foreground are the modest buildings of a small shipyard with one schooner under construction and another ready for launching; in the Bay eight two-masted schooners can be counted. [NATIONAL MARITIME MUSEUM, SAN FRANCISCO].

Mexico carrying general cargoes, although lumber provided a regular trade to many.

Three-masted schooners, some of them terns, continued to be built in varying sizes in every year with an especial boom in the period 1916–20. The last three-master, according to John Lyman, was the *Adams* built in 1929 at Essex, Massachusetts, of 370 tons.

Many of the terns built in Nova Scotia in the First World War boom period were designed on sharp lines, some being given a clipper bow and others a round bow similar to the fishing schooners. More than 150 were launched in 1918 and 1919. In *American Sailing Craft*, Howard I. Chapelle gives the lines of the tern schooner *Marjory Mahaffy*, constructed in 1919 by John McLean & Sons at Mahone Bay,

Nova Scotia, and the plan shows great deadrise with a long convex entrance and a hollow run, with a deep drag aft. She was 130ft 3in long and had a reputation for speed, being heavily rigged with long gaffs. Schooners such as this brought salt from the West Indies and in turn took away salt fish to the Mediterranean, West Indies and South America.

The last Nova-Scotian cargo-carrying schooner was the *Mary B. Brooks*, begun in 1920 but not completed until 1926.

On the Pacific Coast of America, shipbuilding activity was sparked off by the gold discovery of 1849 and there was an immediate demand for small vessels to transport people and goods around the San Francisco Bay area and up the rivers. Of course there were no shipyards in existence but amongst those who had flocked there to make their fortunes were shipwrights, and one of these was John G. North, a native of Norway, who opened a shipyard after a few months of mining. In San Francisco he built in 1854 the three-masted schooner *Susan and Kate Deming* which was no mean achievement, because by 1860 only about six vessels of over 100 tons each had been constructed. Four two-masted schooners were built on the West Coast in 1861 and thereafter numbers began to increase with every decade. The first three-masted schooner to be built there of over 300 tons was the *Sunshine* in 1875, and the

Launch of the tern schooner B. R. Tower *in 1920 from a small yard at the mouth of the Diligent River, Nova Scotia. She was of 343 tons and had a length of 140 feet. She was wrecked two years later.* [NOVA SCOTIA MUSEUM, HALIFAX].

first one of over 400 tons was the *William Renton* in 1882. It is thanks to the researches of the late John Lyman that it is possible to write with certainty of such records.

In 1864 the ex-barge *Victoria* was re-built as a four-masted schooner of 344 tons at San Francisco. Next in date comes the *Novelty* in 1886 but she was given four pole masts on a steamer's hull. The next year, there were three proper schooners, the *Kitsap*, *Volunteer* and *Wm. F. Vitzemann*. For the rest of the century, sizes of four-masters were generally in the 550–750 tons range and the first of over 1000 tons, the *Rosamund*, did not appear until 1900. The first five-masted schooner was the *Louis* of 1888 and 831 tons, but she had a steamer's hull; the first five-master built as a real schooner was the *Inca* of 1014 tons, built at Port Blakely, Washington, in 1896.

Square topsails were continued for much longer than on the East Coast and the four-masters generally carried a fore yard from which a square sail could be set with raffees above it on either side of the topmast. Another West Coast feature was the setting of a leg-of-mutton sail on the aftermost mast instead of a gaff sail, together with a topsail in the shape of a staysail hoisted from the boom end to the topmast head. This was locally called a 'ringtail'. The first authenticated case of this, wrote John

Deck view of the three-masted schooner William Bisbee *looking aft towards the poop. The great beam, wide decks, massive bulwark stanchions, raised quarter deck surrounding an after deckhouse are alien to British eyes but typical of American vessels. She was built in 1902 at Rockland, Maine, 309 tons gross with a length of 133.1 feet and a beam of 31.2 feet.* [W. J. LEWIS PARKER].

With long bowsprits and jibbooms projecting over the wharf, lumber schooners lie in tiers at Havana. Lumber was dragged over the bows along chutes, three of which can be seen in the centre of the picture. [NATIONAL MARITIME MUSEUM, SAN FRANCISCO].

Lyman, was the two-masted schooner *Rosario* in 1879. Even the big four and five-masted schooners used this rig.

Many of the later hulls were built to stand up without ballast and had only one continuous deck; there were a few hold beams but no laid 'tween decks, and longitudinal strength was obtained by providing excessively deep keelsons and by bilge stringers worked into the ceiling, see illustration on page 117.

The barquentine rig was very popular on the West Coast even though the cost of the masts and yards on the foremast equalled the cost of all the other masts put together. The hulls usually had sharp ends and they could outsail the schooners; for long Pacific voyages the square canvas on one mast was ideal, and some schooners were converted to this rig.

Halfway through the first decade of the twentieth century, the construction of four and three-masted schooners virtually ceased on the West Coast until the time of the First World War, when a series of events occurred in 1916 which produced a shipbuilding boom. This was largely confined to vessels of over 1000 tons with four or five masts. The last three-master, the auxiliary *Doris Crane*, was built in 1920.

CHAPTER TEN

Victorian Schooners

In the twenty odd years between the end of the Napoleonic Wars and the accession
to the throne of the young Queen Victoria, the shape and appearance of the British
schooner barely altered. Most were heavily rigged with a considerable amount of
square canvas on the foremast which put them into the category of 'schooner-
brigantines' as described in Chapter Seven. Some of these were built on fine lines
but many were full-bodied and little different from coasting brigs or cutters in the
packet service. A few open-decked boats, working in tidal rivers or estuaries, were
schooner-rigged in these years according to the evidence of prints and paintings.

*An unknown schooner preparing to anchor in Falmouth Bay. With a light wind astern and square
topsails still set, the mainsail and all but one of the headsails have been lowered, but not stowed. The
peak of the foresail has been dropped to spill the wind from the sail, and the anchor is acockbill with
the flukes just under the surface, ready for dropping. Two of the crew can be made out near the
windlass to ensure that the chain runs out smoothly.* [OSBORNE STUDIOS].

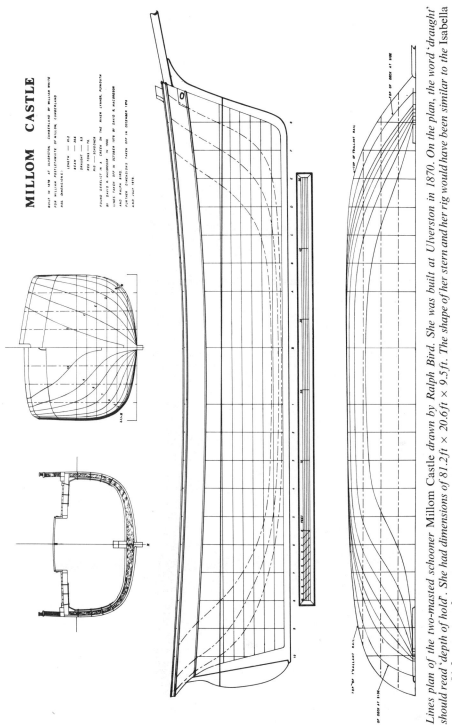

MILLOM CASTLE

BUILT IN 1870 AT ULVERSTON, CUMBERLAND, BY WILLIAM WHITE
FOR WILLIAM POSTLETHWAITE OF MILLOM, CUMBERLAND.

REG. DIMENSIONS: LENGTH ——— 81.2
BEAM ——— 20.6
DRAUGHT ——— 9.5
REG. TONS ——— 74
RIG — SCHOONER

FOUND DERELICT IN A CREEK ON THE RIVER LYNHER, PLYMOUTH
BY DAVID R. MACGREGOR IN 1960.

LINES TAKEN OFF IN OCTOBER 1978 BY DAVID R. MACGREGOR
AND RALPH BIRD.

FURTHER DIMENSIONS TAKEN OFF IN DECEMBER 1978
AND JULY 1979.

TOP OF TRANSOM

TOP OF DECK AT SIDE

TOP OF TRANSOM RAIL

TOP OF DECK AT SIDE

TOP OF TRANSOM RAIL

Lines plan of the two-masted schooner Millom Castle drawn by Ralph Bird. She was built at Ulverston in 1870. On the plan, the word 'draught' should read 'depth of hold'. She had dimensions of 81.2ft × 20.6ft × 9.5ft. The shape of her stern and her rig would have been similar to the Isabella on page 81. [RALPH BIRD].

The three-masted schooner Silvia *under sail in a fresh breeze. This is almost certainly the vessel built at Appledore in 1871 by William Pickard of 164 tons, because the only other schooner of this name in* Lloyd's Register *was a French vessel spelled* Sylvia *(1869). The* Silvia *began life as a two-master owned at Hull, but she was a three-master by 1896. The gaff jaws of the foresail are well below the hounds because a reef has been taken in the sail.* [NEPTUNE PUBLICATIONS].

Remarkably enough, the sail plan of a merchant schooner drawn to scale, was published in 1830 by the naval architect Peter Hedderwick and from evidence in his text she can be identified as the *Glasgow* built in 1826 of 155 tons. She has a little deadrise, round bilges, full entrance and run, square stern, heavy head and trail boards, and a flush deck. This was the current style. The sail plan is very detailed and portrays a schooner with a rig that was used quite extensively in northern Europe in which the topsail yard slid on the doubling of the topmast; above it was the topgallant, each with its own stunsail. Possibly by 1840, the hull-form was getting a little less bluff, particularly in the run, but the most notable change would have been the decrease in the depth of hold, due to the fact that a vessel's depth was actually being measured to calculate the tonnage. This amazing event became law in 1836, it having been assumed prior to this that the depth was merely half the breadth, and everyone took advantage of the fact. So hulls became shallower and therefore carried less

The 100-ton schooner Louise *completed at Clement's shipyard and ready for launching into the River Gannel at Tregunnel near Newquay in 1877. The yard was on the shore line and the tide has even lapped the keel blocks.* [RICHARD GILLIS COLLECTION].

cargo unless they were made longer, a proportion which increased their speed potential. The full-bodied hulls needed large sail plans to drive them along.

Schooners were becoming more popular after 1840 because they were cheaper to build and rig than brigs and required a smaller crew, and because of this there were smaller running expenses. Simultaneously greater attention was being given to design – 'symmetry' was the popular word – and there was even a hint of finer-lined hulls. How far the influence of clipper schooners spilled into the building of everyday schooners is hard to assess, but they were undoubtedly discussed, and competition with railways and steamers certainly affected schooners in the coasting trades.

Contemporary books on sailmaking and rigging give few direct references on how to tackle a schooner in about 1850 and are still obsessed with a square-rigged foremast. The schooner-brigantine described in a previous chapter is still much in evidence in books by Robert Kipping and George Biddlecombe, as well as in Arthur Young's *Nautical Dictionary*.

Schooners were very busy in the fruit trade, and in *The Merchant Schooners* Basil Greenhill has given some interesting statistics relating to it. In 1854 there were 70

The Englishman *of Lancaster is here seen leaving Holyhead in 1932; the mizen has not yet been hoisted and one of the crew is standing beneath the sail on top of the wheel house. Built in 1864 at Glasson Dock near Lancaster by Matthew Simpson, the* Englishman *was of 118 tons net and was originally a two-master, the mizen not being added until after 1900.* [DAVID CLEMENT COLLECTION].

A stern view of the topgallant schooner Lord Devon *on the fore shore in Salcombe. She was built in 1885 at Salcombe of 98 tons and was copper sheathed.* [FAIRWEATHER COLLECTION].

Schooners in the harbour of Port St Mary, Isle of Man, at low water. Nearest is the Margaret Garton, *built in 1877 at the port, and astern is the* Venus, *built at Perth in 1876.* [DAVID CLEMENT COLLECTION].

schooners involved in carrying the 60 million oranges and 15 million lemons exported from the Azores and western Mediterranean to London alone, and altogether 240 schooners were engaged in the trade. Pineapples were brought from the West Indies by schooner; melons came from Portugal, and currants and other dried fruit from the eastern Mediterranean.

Before steam competition got too intense, schooners were employed in the packet trades carrying passengers and light package goods between Scotland and the north of England to London. They were also used on the Waterford to Bristol run and likewise to the Channel Islands. From these islands, fresh vegetables and new potatoes were brought up Channel to Southampton and London during the fifties and sixties.

But schooners were in regular trade around the coastline of the British Isles, carrying cargoes from port to port right up to 1914, and also in the 'home trade', that is to say to the Continent between the River Elbe and Brest. There was coal from north-east England, manure from London, china clay from Devon, slate from North Wales, iron ore from Cumberland to name but a fraction of the interchange of com-

Three square-sterned topsail schooners crossing Mount's Bay, Cornwall, on the starboard tack. The schooner on the right is still hoisting her upper topsail. [F. E. GIBSON].

modities. The same schooners that were working coastwise might also pick up a charter to go to the Baltic for timber, or other cargoes in the home trade. There were also regular deep-water trades such as the carriage of salted cod from Newfoundland across the Atlantic to Spain, Portugal and Italy, or to South America; other schooners even made the long perilous voyage around Cape Horn to load copper ore in Chile.

The rise and fall of the tide had a strong influence on the design of schooners because unless they could remain constantly afloat they required the ability to sit moderately upright on the bottom at low water as the tide ebbed away. In the Baltic, the Mediterranean, American ports south of Boston, and in equatorial zones, the rise and fall of the tide was small or negligible, and vessels with steep deadrise could remain permanently afloat. In Great Britain, northern Europe and the Maritime Provinces of Canada, vessels would have to take the ground twice-a-day unless they could lie in

A scene at Blakeney at the turn of the century: a fishing smack on the left; and on the right the schooner Minstrel *of 66 tons, built at Wells in 1847; beyond her are the masts of the billy boy* Blue Jacket. [MACGREGOR COLLECTION].

one of the few docks with lock gates. At most harbours in the British Isles, brigs and brigantines, schooners, ketches, smacks and barges could be seen at low water in various ungainly positions, and woe betide the skipper or mate who had not taken the right precautions. A craft with steep deadrise, unless secured beside a quay, would just lie on her side and might not rise as the tide flooded.

William Trebilcock remembers how, in the trading smack *Mary*, they were lying at Penryn loading cargo from the flat-bottomed schooner *Millom Castle*. As the tide rose so did the *Mary* but the half-empty *Millom Castle* did not. Only when the water was within a foot of her deck did she suddenly rise up out of the water like a whale, breaking the suction of the Penryn mud, her rigging slatting to and fro. Expecting trouble, a crew sometimes passed chains around the hull which could be pulled up and down to break the suction.

So schooners had to be built with little or no deadrise, but they could have sharp ends to achieve speed. There were really two basic forms of hull in the second half of the nineteenth century: one was put into fast-sailing craft and consisted of a long convex entrance with almost vertical bow sections, together with a long and concave run; the other, normally intended for vessels where cargo capacity was the prime consideration, had more balanced ends, possibly even with hollows in the fore-body but certainly hollow aft. Perhaps the first full-form, to be found especially in Devon and Cornwall, owes its origin to the fast-sailing cutters of the eighteenth century, while the other style is a scaled-down version of a brig. Plans I have drawn out and published of the Brixham-built *Fling* (1858) or the Cornish *Rhoda Mary* (1868) are of the first-named hull-form; the Aberdeen brigantine *Juan de la Vega* (1871) or the Glasson-built *Express* (1860) are of the other kind.

Deck layouts did not vary much from one schooner to another although they differed endlessly in detail. The windlass for heaving in the anchor was always a wooden barrel with an 'Armstrong patent' apparatus for revolving it, and it was situated up in the bows. The scuttle to the crew's accommodation below deck was close abaft the windlass. Next came the fore hatch, followed by the foremast, galley, main hatch – on top of which was the longboat in chocks – mainmast, pumps and fife rail, after hatch, skylight to the cabin, companion to the after accommodation, with finally binnacle and wheel. In a three-masted schooner, the mizen would be stepped between the after hatch and the skylight.

Decks were sometimes holystoned to a light creamy colour, but many schooners painted theirs red or blue; bulwarks were frequently white inside with mouldings and rail picked out in colour; masts, yards, gaffs and booms were often varnished but the masts up to the height of the boom chocks were often red, blue or green with deck fittings, or at least the ironwork, to match. Galley, companion and other wooden fittings were either varnished or painted or were a combination of the two. Externally, hulls were almost invariably black with a white or gold band at the sheer strake that ran up to the top edge of the trail board carving; sometimes the rail was white too. A good way to tell if a schooner was going 'foreign' would be the copper sheathing on her bottom below the load waterline, designated in *Lloyd's Register* by the letters 'Y.M.' Painted ports were met with infrequently and then only on the longer schooners.

Under tow in the Avon gorge, bound into Bristol from Cueta Vechia, the William Morton *was photographed by W. A. Sharman on 4 August 1915. She was a Western Ocean Yacht having been built at Portmadoc by David Jones in 1905 of 143 tons. She was abandoned at sea in 1919. She still has stunsail booms on her lower yard.* [DAVID CLEMENT COLLECTION].

Schooners in Europe, both in Great Britain and on the Continent, almost invariably carried square sails on the foremast so that the term 'schooner' automatically assumes this fact; indeed, if square sails were absent, the term 'fore-and-aft schooner' had to be used to note the difference. Conversely in America, a schooner was automatically deemed to be fore-and-aft rigged and so the presence of square canvas on the foremast drew the term 'topsail schooner'. Sometimes schooners in Europe that carried topgallants were called 'topgallant yard schooners'.

Although the square sails were regularly set, the gaff sails were the largest sails. Double topsails did not replace the single ones until the 1880's at which time older vessels often did away with the topgallant. A square sail was often set below the fore lower yard in favourable winds, and there were probably four headsails; in addition, there was a fore-and-aft main topsail and a main topmast staysail. Stunsails were carried until the end of the seventies, although a few deepwater schooners retained them, and they have been photographed on some of John Stephens' vessels.

The steel-hulled C. &. F. Nurse *heeling over in a fresh breeze on the starboard tack with all sail set. The yards are braced sharp up. She was built at Falmouth in 1900 by William H. Lean for the Nurse family of Bridgwater.* [DAVID CLEMENT COLLECTION].

(Above left) *Most of the schooners and ketches continued to use deadeyes and lanyards instead of bottle screws for setting up their rigging, and here two men from the yard of P. K. Harris & Sons are attending to the main rigging of the ketch* Democrat *at Appledore in May 1951.* [AUTHOR].

(Above right) *Looking down on to the fore deck of the ketch* Irene *at Appledore in June 1954. The layout was similar in many schooners.* [AUTHOR].

Later in the century, some of the schooners were built with round sterns but the majority always had square ones. However there was a form of round stern that was in existence from earlier times, colloquially called the 'Irish Sea stern' because it was mostly found on vessels built in yards bordering this Sea. Such a hull was double-ended with the rudder head outside the hull and the entire stern was framed with cant timbers, as at the bow, thus removing the need for overhanging counter timbers and transoms. It resulted in a very strong structure. The Dutch had found it successful in the flutes, and the billy-boys on the north-east coast also used it. Basil Greenhill has suggested in *The Merchant Schooners* that it developed from the river barges of the Mersey. Or it could have evolved from the 'galliot' which was used in north-west England and which was described in 1846 as 'a flat-bottomed vessel whose bow and stern are similar, being round and bluff'.

Appledore men disparagingly called them 'Barrow flats', but they had several advantages: they were of shallow draft, sailed on an almost even keel, were good sea boats, could sail without ballast, were cheap to build and immensely strong. An example of this hull-form is to be found in the *Millom Castle* which has survived deeply embedded in the mud of the Lynher River. I found the hull in August 1960 but there was no name on her. Subsequently I reported this find to the late Cmdr H. Oliver Hill who was eventually able to identify her. Before she disintegrated too much, Ralph Bird and I were able to take off her lines and he has reconstructed a fine plan, reproduced here, from which it can be seen that she had 20 feet of dead-flats amidships.

The splendid quality of her pitch pine planking, both externally and in the ceiling, has held her together, and there are few butt joints to be found. According to the

Melancholy end to the Susan Elizabeth *at St. Ives. She had been built as a cutter at Salcombe in 1857, but was rebuilt ten years later when she was presumably re-rigged as a schooner of 70 tons.* [F. E. GIBSON].

The crew takes a well-earned rest aboard the M. A. James *at Padstow in the 1930s whilst unloading coal. The master, George Slade, is second from the left. This three-masted schooner was built at Portmadoc in 1900 as a Western Ocean yacht and survived the Second World War.* [MACGREGOR COLLECTION].

Aboard the Result *in August 1948 as she lay beside the quay at Fremington, North Devon. The hatch covers have been removed so that unloading her coal cargo can begin the next morning.* [AUTHOR].

Lloyd's Register survey report, the keelson and rider keelson, both of pitch pine, have no scarphs and so are each presumably in one piece from stem to stern. The frames are of oak, nearly all the sixteen deck beams are of larch and the deck planking is yellow pine. Lloyd's Register classed her 10A1 and she was of 91 tons. Forming one of the fleet of twenty-eight vessels owned in the seventies by William Postlethwaite of Barrow, she was designed to carry cargoes of iron ore and coal from the Cumberland and Lancashire mines.

Not many schooners were built of iron because it required a shipyard with reasonably sophisticated equipment for bending the frames and plates, and such yards usually concentrated on larger sailing vessels or on steamers. But Alexander Stephen & Sons and Denny Bros built some on the Clyde. Stephen's first schooner was the two-master *Angelita* built in 1859 of 129 tons and 100 ft long, with a deep narrow hull having six beams to her length. She 'careened in launching' noted Stephen in his diary, probably meaning that she fell over on her side as she went down the ways.

The three-masted schooner Bessie *of Salcombe in Dover Harbour after a collision in the 1880s. The bowsprit has gone and so has most of the cutwater and head knees. She had been built at Kingsbridge in 1871. Note the iron cathead.* [RICHARD GILLIS COLLECTION].

Unloading cargo from the three-masted schooner Mary Barrow *into a cart at Custom House Quay, Falmouth. The checker-board pattern is painted on the trail boards.* [OSBORNE STUDIOS].

She was built for the copper ore trade around Cape Horn. Their second schooner was the three-masted *Metero* of 191 tons built in 1866 of composite construction with shallow draft and large beam, and altogether a surprising hull-form to send around Cape Horn. Perhaps the fact that she stranded off Valparaiso on her maiden passage indicates that she possessed insufficient weatherly qualities. One would have expected a centreboard for a depth of hold of only 9 ft with a beam of 26 ft, but centreboards were only rarely fitted in Great Britain because regularly taking the ground in drying harbours caused them to get jammed with debris.

However, one of Denny's schooners, the *Annsbro'* of 105 tons built in 1846, had a five-sided centreboard pivoting on the keelson, according to a lines plan in the National Maritime Museum. She is flat-floored with sharp ends and is heavily rigged with a fore royal yard and even lower stunsails beside the square sail from the fore yard. Here are two examples of centreboards being removed: when the iron sloop *Clipper* (1844) was re-rigged as a schooner in 1847, her 'sliding keel' was removed; in 1857 the three-masted schooner *Phantom* of 210 tons, built four years earlier at New York, had hers removed at Appledore.

Unlike the United States, the size of schooners did not increase dramatically as the century wore on, and the only noticeable alteration was the insertion of a third mast.

When there was no quay, cargoes were unloaded straight into carts on the beach, as here on the Percuel River near St. Mawes. A stage has been rigged over the side and carts take their turn to be loaded. A special cargo gaff was kept for such work, and the scene beside this ketch would have been repeated in schooners and smacks. On the right is the landing stage for the ferry and a donkey and cart are transferring goods, and another is waiting. The deck layout corresponds to that on a two-masted schooner. [RALPH BIRD].

The word 'insertion' is used deliberately as many two-masters reduced their extremely long main booms by half, and added a mizen mast. Frequently the mainmast did not have to be shifted. Simultaneously, the fore topgallant was discarded and the single topsail replaced by double ones on a shortened fore topmast. The schooners built towards the end of the nineteenth century became somewhat longer but fuller-bodied amidships, although few were built with any real parallel middle body.

But in the North Atlantic trade there was room for improvement and a breed of fine three-masted schooners was developed which earned the name of 'Western Ocean Yachts'. The export of salt cod from Labrador and Newfoundland was an ancient one and due to the smallness of many of the settlements at which the fish was cleaned, salted and laid out to dry, only small vessels were of use.

In the 1860s fruit schooners were being chartered for Atlantic voyages from Brixham and Salcombe. It was a hard slog to windward and the toast 'Forty days to the westward!' epitomized the hard driving masters intent on making a fast passage. Many vessels took months to sail across and only the finest schooners were employed. By contrast, once loaded, they sped before the westerlies bound for European ports

With canvas reduced to foresail and one headsail, and with the help of her engine, the Isabella *makes her way into Newlyn harbour. This schooner with her 'Irish Sea stern' was built at Barrow by Ashburner in 1878 of 75 tons net. She should not be confused with the schooner of the same name which was built at Galmpton above Dartmouth in 1864 by Gibbs and owned in Fowey by John Stephens.* [JOHN MUNN].

The Mary Rosanna *has a tall enough fore topmast to set a royal. She was built at Ardrossan in 1860 of 87 tons.* [MacGregor collection].

and often made the crossing in less than twenty days, several taking under two weeks. Some schooners made only one or two round trips per year but others built specifically for the trade were sailing continuously back and forth even in the winter. This was a really hard life for a vessel of 150 tons or so.

The principal ports from which the schooners sailed were Portmadoc and Fowey, and the trade was at its height in the years 1880 to 1910. John Stephens of Fowey owned a large fleet in the trade, many rigged as schooners, of which he was very proud. In 1895 his *Spinaway* took 15 days between St John's and Oporto; in 1896 the *Little Secret* sailed from Trinidad to Gibraltar in 17 days. Perhaps it was after her arrival on this passage or else another the same year that Heywood's Branch of the Bank of Liverpool wrote to the Credit Lyonnais in London on 1 February 1896 requesting them 'to give bail for the sum of £1500 to the Government Authority of Bilbao guaranteeing payment of duties in respect of a cargo of Codfish by the vessel *Little Secret* consigned to Alloqui for account of C. T. Bowring & Co of Liverpool...' Long-hand copies were made of all letters sent from offices and the post was so rapid that business could be quickly expedited.

The 'Western Ocean Yachts' were really those sailing from Portmadoc in the thirty or so years before the First World War and were built specifically for the arduous Newfoundland trade. They were lofty three-masted schooners carrying double topsails and a topgallant on a tall fore topmast, four headsails on a high-steeved bow-sprit, with high narrow gaff sails. Using the lines of the *M. A. James* as a guide, the hulls possessed a big sheer with a short convex entrance and a longer somewhat hollow run with powerful quarters; the midship breadth was kept well forward, and the whole body of the ship narrowed-in from the mainmast to the square stern, thus minimizing the width of the square stern at the end of the long counter. The *M. A. James* cost £2000 to construct and equip or £16.12 per ton on 124.07 gross tons. Basil Greenhill has estimated that there were about fifty schooners of this type built either at Portmadoc or elsewhere.

The First World War changed everything. Steam coasters, the internal combustion engine, and the spreading railways concentrated cargo-handling in the larger ports and closed down the smaller ones. Horse-drawn carts no longer queued up beside Blakeney Quay, nor were they driven on to the wet sand of St Ives harbour at low water when coal was being discharged from ketches and schooners. Economy was the watchword and auxiliary diesel engines were being installed everywhere, lofty spars shortened and crews reduced in number.

Before closing this chapter, mention should be made of the few four-masted

Two of the crew of the ketch Agnes *heaving up and down on the handles of the Armstrong patent windlass to heave in the anchor cable. This tedious back-breaking task had been repeated in countless schooners with identical apparatus over the previous hundred years and yet it has been rarely photographed.* [AUTHOR].

ALL SAILS STORED AT OWNER'S RISK

H. S. PRIOR,

SAIL MAKER.

AWNING, BLIND & COVER MAKER.

PHONE : 705.

CHURCH STREET,

FALMOUTH.

(At rear National & Provincial Bank)

Flying Jib 67 yds
Boom Foresail 166 yds
Fore Staysail 84 yds
Squaresail 98 yds.
Mainsail 212 yds Twine
Standing Jib 54 yds Twine
Boom Jib 66 yds Twine
Gaff Topsail. 80 to 90 yds

about sizes for
Katie Schooner

1,000

7/6

List of sail areas for the two-masted schooner Katie *probably prepared about 1930. The dimensions will be 'running' yards of canvas, 21 in wide, and not areas.* [MacGREGOR COLLECTION].

schooners built in Great Britain. Two were built of steel in Scotland for Hawaiian registry, the *Americana* in 1892 and the *Honolulu* in 1896. The latter was a bald-headed fore-and-after of 1080 tons. The *Americana* of 901 tons was built for the lumber trade and according to a photograph in the *American Neptune* (vol II) was first rigged with topmasts on each mast, a single lower yard on the foremast, but also a lower yard and double topsail yards on the mainmast. Built the same year as *Americana* was the four-masted *Rimac* of 858 tons probably first rigged as a topgallant schooner, but four years later altered to the same sort of rig as *Americana*. Reid of Port Glasgow who built her had constructed the steel *Tacora* in 1888 as a four-masted topgallant yard schooner of 828 tons, but re-rigged her later as a barquentine.

Steel three-masted schooners had of course been built of which the *Result* (1892) is a survivor being now preserved near Belfast. In the Richmond Yard at Appledore, James and Frank Cock constructed four steel three-masted schooners in the period 1904—9, and all of about 99 tons net.

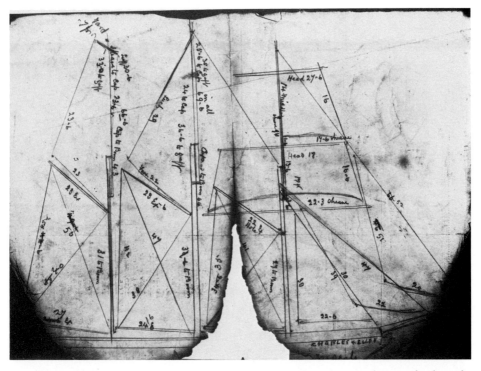

Sail plan of the Charles & Ellen *drawn on the back of a Falmouth poster bearing the date of 6 January 1916, and found in Penrose's sail loft. Prior & Holdroff were previously the sailmakers in that loft. This schooner dropped out of the Mercantile Navy List between 1917 and 1919. She had been built as a two-master at Barrow in 1878 by D. Noble & Co having been built of iron with dimensions of 106.2ft × 22.6ft × 10.5ft and 145 tons. It is interesting that iron schooners were longer in relation to their beam than wooden schooners, as instanced by the wooden* Margaret Hobley *which was also owned by William Postlethwaite and which had almost identical breadth and depth of hold measurements to the* Charles & Ellen, *yet was almost exactly 20ft shorter.* [MACGREGOR COLLECTION].

CHAPTER ELEVEN

Yachts

Yachts rigged as schooners were amongst the largest vessels used for pleasure and so this form of sport permitted comparatively few men to indulge in it, even in a period like the nineteenth century when wages and running costs were minimal. George H. Ackers, a member of the Royal Yacht Squadron from 1837 to 1871, must have liked schooners because he owned, first the two-masted *Dolphin* which had topsails and topgallants on both masts; then for twenty-three years he had the three-masted schooner *Brilliant* of 393 tons which had four yards on two masts and at one time had them on each mast. Many members of the Squadron owned schooner yachts in the 80 to 200 tons range.

The schooner Westward *between the 'J'-class gaff cutters;* Lulworth *(left) and* Britannia. *The* Westward, *ex* Hamburg II, *ex* Westward *was designed and built by Herreshoff at Bristol, Rhode Island, in 1910 and was raced in Britain by T. B. F. Davis. She registered 180 tons gross or 323 tons T.M. and was 135 ft long overall.* [OSBORNE STUDIOS].

Schooner Yacht "AMERICA"

Rigging Plan as between 1851 –1859

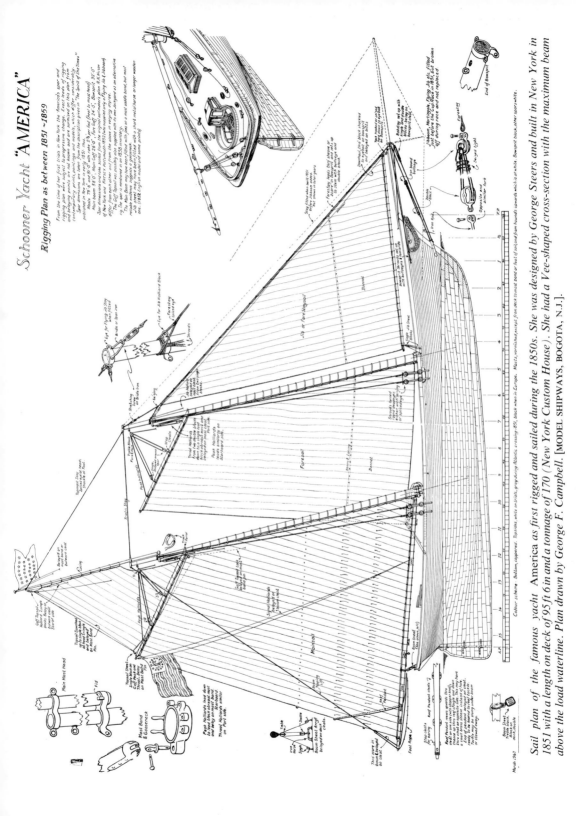

From the time of her first trials in New York the America's spar and rigging plan were subject to progressive changes, and the details of rigging points overlaid herein and are summised on this plan. From contemporary prints, paintings and models, which differ considerably.

Spar dimensions are taken from the description given in "The Field of the Times," published in New York in 1851, thus:—

Masts 79'6 and 81'0 with rake 2⅜ per foot (fore to most bend)

Main boom 58'0, Main Gaff 26'0, Fore Gaff 24'0, Bowsprit 32'0

Spar dimensions overtaken asisted from the original contemporary plan of the New York built America in 1851 at her mouth with flying jib (kitchen) differ from each other and some are on varying charter.

The Gaff Topsail was possibly still supplied with its own dedegeared as an alternative rig. The spar is mentioned in an 1858 inventory.

The Main Boom may have been fitted with a mast saddle bend, but most reliable evidence suggests a gooseneck.

Jib sheet may have been fitted with a short metal horse or longer wooden one. (1858 rigs is made and some points)

Sail plan of the famous yacht America as first rigged and sailed during the 1850s. She was designed by George Steers and built in New York in 1851 with a length on deck of 95 ft 6 in and a tonnage of 170 (New York Custom House). She had a Vee-shaped cross-section with the maximum beam above the load waterline. Plan drawn by George F. Campbell. [MODEL SHIPWAYS, BOGOTA, N.J.]

Colour scheme. Bottom, coppered. Topsides, white on trials, grey during Atlantic crossing 1851, black when in Europe. Masts, varnished except from deck to mast band or fast of sail (and from hounds upwards which is all white. Bowsprit black, other spars white.

March 1967

The appearance of the yacht *America* in 1851 did have a profound effect on British yacht design and many hastened to copy her or make the bows of their yachts more hollow like hers. It also popularized the schooner rig on yachts. Her designer, George Steers, had previously designed other fast schooner yachts as well as pilot boats. Schooner yachts in America, however, were not unduly influenced by the *America*. In British waters, races between schooners became popular. In December 1866 three American yachts, the *Henrietta*, *Vesta* and *Fleetwing* raced across the Atlantic for a stake of £10,000, which the *Henrietta* won with a time of 13 days 21 hours between Sandy Hook and Cowes.

The British schooner *Cambria* and the American *Sappho* raced in 1868 and 1870. By this date, racing schooners were only rigged with fore-and-aft canvas although cruising yachts continued to set square sails on the foremast. There were a small number of big three-masted cruising yachts such as *Sunbeam*, *Czarina* and *Aello II* but they usually had auxiliary engines. The *Sunbeam* made a celebrated voyage round the world in 1876–77, her longest day's run under sail alone being 270 miles in the South Atlantic. Another favourite cruising ground was in Arctic waters. *Hunt's Universal Yacht List* is a useful compendium as it gives the sailmaker's names, house

The fore-and-aft schooner yacht Janette *off the Eddystone lighthouse. Her fore yard to set a square sail is lowered close to the deck. Perhaps she was owned by the 5th Earl of Egremont in the 1840's.* [PARKER GALLERY].

The three-masted schooner Brilliant *was sailed by George H. Ackers from 1839 to 1862 and this wash drawing depicts guns run out, naval fashion. Various tonnages are assigned to her, but her register tons was 292; 393 was possibly o.m. tons, and 480 in Hunts Yacht List was presumably Thames Measurement. Her builder was Rubie. This type of rig was given occasionally to merchant schooners both in Britain and Northern Europe.* [MACGREGOR COLLECTION].

flags, dates when altered and clubs as well as the usual measurements. Many of the schooners had long lives and one of the largest schooners afloat in 1905 without auxiliary engines was probably *Livonia* of 128 tons built in 1871 as challenger for the 'America's Cup'.

Since 1918 schooner yachts have been built in limited numbers, although usually in smaller sizes and particularly in America. In the 1970s old Baltic galleases have been refitted in Great Britain, some of them with schooner rig. In the United States, schooners have always been popular as yachts, whether small or large and the gaff has remained in favour. Some replicas have latterly been built such as the topsail schooner *Shenandoah* in 1964, based on the Customs cutter *Joe Lane* of 1849. Ports such as Camden, Maine, have quite a fleet of bald-headed 'dude' schooners for holiday cruises afloat. A replica of the famous *America* was produced in 1967 at a cost of half-a-million dollars which was twenty-five times the cost of the original.

The Morwenna *under full sail almost becalmed. Built at Shoreham by Stow & Son in 1914 and designed by Linton Hope, she was still being sailed by Mr. I. T. Barling and his family after the last War.* [I. M. BARLING].

In this dramatic picture of the power of wind-filled canvas, the American schooner-yacht Dauntless *has a quartering wind. Built in 1869 at Mystic, Connecticut, by Forsyth she measured 116.7ft × 24.7ft × 9.7ft and 299 tons Thames Measurement. The big square sail is sheeted to a boom and there are four headsails.* [BEKEN & SON].

Looking aft aboard the Morwenna *with the owner standing on the companion stairs. This schooner was built of wood with an overall length of 55 ft and a Thames measurement tonnage of 28 and gross tonnage of 20.* [I. M. BARLING].

Schooner Vema, *ex* Hussar IV, *was built in Copenhagen in 1923 for Edward F. Hutton of New York and was renowned for her speed. All Hutton's yachts appear to have been named* Hussar, *and this one was sold in the 1930s and renamed. Hutton's famous four-masted barque bearing the same name appeared in 1931. The schooner pictured here was built of steel with a gross tonnage of 533 and an overall length of 196.6 ft; she had diesel engines.* [MACGREGOR COLLECTION].

CHAPTER TWELVE

Schooners in Europe

Although the schooner rig started in Holland in the early part of the seventeenth century, it appears to have gone out of favour in the eighteenth century because, out of the eighty-four engravings of various rigs published by G. Groenewegen at Rotterdam in 1789, only one depicts a schooner, a *Kanonneer boot*, with square topsails on each mast. Prior to 1815, all illustrations of Dutch schooners show them to be armed.

In the first half of the nineteenth century, North European round-sterned galliots and square-sterned galleases set three square sails on the mainmast – topgallant, topsail and deep squaresail from the lower yard – and also a gaff sail. On the mizen, whose topmast was often as high above the deck as the main topmast, there was a

356 · PAIMPOL · Goëlette Islandaise

A French topsail schooner at Paimpol, Brittany, with every sail set except the fore staysail. The deep fore topsail is a roller-reefing variety, with the sail rolling around a subsidiary yard as the topsail yard is lowered. The name of this schooner is unknown. A few of these schooners had three masts. [MacGREGOR COLLECTION].

One of the four-masted schooners built in Denmark was the Richard *of 325 tons net, constructed at Svendborg of wood in 1920. Seen here in ballast, she made a fine sight with four yards on her foremast.* [F. HOLM-PETERSEN].

narrower gaff sail and a topsail. Schooners had a very similar rig, of course, but with a bigger mainsail. From the plans in Hans Szymanski's book, *Deutsche Segelschiffe*, it can be seen that the galleas and galliot were both full-bodied craft, but that the schooner had a sharper entrance and run. He reproduces a painting of the schooner *Ferdinand* of Stettin (c1820) with topsails and topgallants on each mast, with the topsail yards sliding on the doubling of the topmast below the cap, which was a favourite style in Germany and Denmark. The *schunerbrigg* was popular in both countries and the *George Canning* of Stettin, pictured as entering Palermo in 1834, has a fore royal mast fidded abaft the topgallant mast, but carries a foresail set on gaff and boom with a luff almost as long as on the mainsail. The large square sail set from the foreyard was always a regular sail with one row of reef points and the *Marta* of Flensburg carried one in 1860 together with a stunsail. Several Danish schooners were in the China coast trade during the sixties and seventies.

During the 1860s there were a few experiments with three-masted schooners, and several had square sails on the main topmast as well as on the fore. Two of this rig were the *Familia* of Troense, Denmark, built 1851, and the *Mathilde* of Kiel built in 1863.

In Norway there was a large trade in carrying ice to the southern ports of England,

The Danish Maren *was really a fore-and-aft schooner but did carry a fore yard, which is here lowered. She had an old hull which was constructed in 1815 at Arnis on the River Schlei, now part of Germany, but she was rigged as a* jagt *or sloop. In 1884 she was sold to owners in the Danish island of Aero and six years later was re-rigged as a schooner.* [F. HOLM-PETERSEN].

Becalmed off Le Tréport when in the trade to the Rio Grande is the Danish schooner Hans *which was built in 1907 at Marstal by H. C. Christensen. She measured 114.0 ft × 25.4 ft × 10.7 ft and 161 tons net. She has five headsails set and the square sail is bent to the fore yard. The two white stripes along her sheer strake identify her. She left Rio de Janeiro in 1914 just before the War and after being dismasted in a pampero, was towed back to Hamburg by a tug. She was sold to the West Indies about 1950.* [F. HOLM-PETERSEN].

and to France and Spain as well, and Norwegian schooners were also found on the China coast and in the West Indies.

Two-masted schooners first appeared in considerable numbers in Denmark in the 1850s although most were 'jagt-built' with bluff bows and vertical stems, but the first clipper in the Svendborg area was the *Thurøe* of 1856. Such schooners carried a topgallant yard and regularly set a square sail below the fore yard. Many left their homeland to trade in the West Indies or the China coast where they spent the rest of their lives.

By the 1890s fine three-masted topgallant schooners were being launched from Scandianvian and north European yards and many of them were similar to the Western Ocean Yachts. The Danish schooners of this type crossed four yards on the foremast and were lofty vessels with pronounced sheer, square sterns and clipper bows. They were often broad in the beam with appreciable deadrise and a sharp convex entrance

Captain S. Jürgensen taking a sight aboard the three-masted schooner Frem *which was built at Marstal in 1919 of 119 tons net. She was built for the Newfoundland trade in which at one time 125 Danish schooners were engaged. This photograph was taken at the stern, looking forward to where her square sail is set; she carried no topsail yards.* [F. HOLM-PETERSEN].

The master, mate and crew aboard the three-masted topsail schooner Yrsa. *She was built at Marstal in 1902 of 100 tons net and a length of 90.7 ft. The spurling pipe, through which the chain cable passes down to the chain locker, is situated on the left at the foot of the mainmast. Danish schooners were similar in size to British schooners.* [F. HOLM-PETERSEN].

A Scandinavian schooner drying her sails at anchor off West Appledore, her bows still pointing towards Bideford Bay. She has not yet unloaded her cargo of timber which still encumbers her decks. [MacGregor collection].

Shipyard sail plan of unidentified Danish two-masted topsail schooner entitled 'new schooner' for Christensen, dating from the period 1870-90. Many of the staysails are drawn to indicate the fulness of the sail cloth to be cut; a topmast and lower stunsail are also drawn, but without their booms or yards. [F. HOLM-PETERSEN].

and run. Counter sterns were usually square, but J. Ring Andersen's yard at Svendborg was famous for graceful round counter sterns. A vessel built at Marstal could be recognized anywhere by its plain curved stem, square tuck stern—the lower part of which was varnished—and outside rudder. These schooners often had a standing gaff on the foremast, and the sail was then hooped to both gaff and mast. Frode Holm-Petersen has chronicled the sailing vessels of Denmark in his many books which are well-illustrated and a good source of information.

Apart from their voyages across the North Sea and the North Atlantic, these three-masted schooners were to be found in ports throughout the world. In 1905 the Svendborg schooner *Dagny* called at the Falkland Islands, and two years later the *Dannebrog* was lost off the Brazilian coast. These schooners continued to be built in large numbers up until 1914 and some were even built between the Wars.

Denmark was unique as being the only country outside North America where large numbers of four-masted schooners were constructed beginning in 1913 and finishing in 1924. In these years, according to a list in *Log Chips* compiled by Jens Malling, no less than fifty-one four-masters were launched, the majority being in 1919 and

In this postcard of Menton there are three schooners lying at anchor in the harbour: that on the left is pole-masted; that on the right is a topsail schooner. In the centre is a three-masted topsail schooner with a double-ended hull and outside rudder. Her name board on her starboard quarter reads: 'Anna Madre Genova'. The first word is in doubt owing to shadows falling across the letters and she has not been positively identified, but her port of register is, in English, Genoa. The Bureau Veritas 'Register' for 1906 and 1910 has no such vessel but the 'Repertoire General' for 1921 has a single vessel named Anna Madre—a schooner with two masts, built of wood in 1906 of 62 tons gross and registered at Livorno (Leghorn). But she looks an interesting vessel. [MacGREGOR COLLECTION].

The three-masted topsail schooner Penola *ex* Naraho *in dry dock on the River Tyne. This vessel was built at Kerity, France, in 1908 and became registered in London about 1934 when her name must have been altered. By 1937 she was owned in South Australia and had 100 BHP engines with tonnages of 138 net and 166 gross and dimensions of 108.0 ft × 24.1 ft × 11.6 ft. By 1939 she was owned in Northumberland and the net tonnage was now 84. Her bow would appear to be strengthened against ice.* [PETERSEN COLLECTION, SOUTH SHIELDS PUBLIC LIBRARIES AND MUSEUMS].

The staysail schooner Stormie Seas, *49 ft long, was used by Peter Throckmorton for exploration in the Mediterranean.* [P. THROCKMORTON].

1920. Seventeen were of steel, the remainder of wood; thirty-four had auxiliary engines; and the majority were in the 300 to 460 tons range. About half-a-dozen carried four yards on the foremast but most only had a single yard on this mast although fidded topmasts were normal.

In Chapter Thirteen there are references to the big American schooners bought by Norwegian owners during the First World War and also to the five-masters ordered by the French Government from the Pacific Coast shipyards.

In France one class of two-masted schooner which resembled the fisherman or *morutier* was the *caboteur* which did not have the deep heel, yet was a fast vessel, being sailed by a crew of five. In rig arrangement she closely resembled the *morutier* with a deep roller-reefing topsail which first made its appearance about 1910. Prior to this, double topsails were set. Although few if any schooners were built after 1914, they can still be remembered under sail in the Bristol Channel in the 1930s when they were taking cargoes of potatoes, onions and pit props to South Wales and returning to Brittany with coal. One which survived the War was the *Roscovite* which lies in Svendborg harbour under the name of *Arken*.

It is difficult to track down all the four or five-masted schooners built in other European countries but the four-master *Abraham* of 315 tons was built at Windau, Russia, in 1893; two five-masters of about 1200 tons each were built in Portugal in

1919, both of wood; two auxiliary four-masters were built in Holland in 1920; and in Italy in 1922 the five-master *Perseveranza* was built of concrete. At Kiel in the same year, Krupp constructed five five-masted schooners, all of which had four yards on the fore and mizen masts, but none on the main, jigger and spanker masts. This rig arrangement made them famous. All were auxiliaries built of steel and all their names ended in 'Vinnen', derived from their owner's name.

In Italy and other Mediterranean countries, the schooner was used extensively in the last century and in this, but picture postcards show that in Italy, especially, the brigantine predominated prior to 1914. At Palma de Majorca, two and three-masted schooners survived into recent years and at least one was constructed as late as 1950. Schooners were still much in use in Greece in 1954 because Basil Greenhill sent me a postcard from Salonica on which he wrote:

'This place is crawling with schooners. There are almost a dozen schooners and smacks in front of the hotel now, and they come and go every hour. Some of them are very attractive and some give the impression of being very new as well. Topsails are definitely *demodé*. The vogue here is for an enormous area of canvas from gaffs and booms from tall rather lovely pole masts. In Syria they go in for very lofty Bermudas.'

There were altogether five schooners of identical rig and size built in 1921-22 by Krupp for the Bremen firm of Vinnen. The names of all five ended in 'Vinnen' but each began with a different Christian name. The register tonnage was 1827 and the dimensions 261.8 ft × 44.3 ft × 19.1 ft, and they all had auxiliary engines. The one pictured here is the Werner Vinnen. *The rig was designed for efficiency in upkeep and manning but a succinct definition of it is lacking.* [DAVID CLEMENT COLLECTION].

CHAPTER THIRTEEN

The Big Schooners

After the American Civil War the shipyards of Maine produced some splendid medium clippers for deepwater trade, later called 'Down Easters', but the high insurance rates decreed by Lloyd's on wooden hulls favoured iron and steel ships, and curtailed the production of square-riggers in Maine after the mid-eighties. So builders and owners turned to the coastwise trade where there was a growing demand for the transport of coal to the manufacturing centres of New England and also of wood for the construction of houses. The scene was now set for the creation of the

The schooner on the left is a typical West Coast lumber schooner named Lottie Bennett, *the leg-of-mutton mainsail on the jigger mast and the 'ringtail' topsail above it being regular features. She was built in 1899 at Port Blakely, Washington, and after twenty years in the lumber business was sold for copra trading in the Pacific. The schooner on the right sets staysails instead of gaff topsails.* [NATIONAL MARITIME MUSEUM, SAN FRANCISCO].

Launch of the Baker Palmer *from the yard of G. L. Weldt at Waldoboro, Maine, in 1901. This three-decked schooner, constructed for the Boston fleet of W. F. Palmer, had a net tonnage of 2240 and dimensions of 284.9 ft × 46.5 ft × 21.9 ft.* [PEABODY MUSEUM, SALEM].

Looking forward aboard the four-masted schooner Wm. J. Lermond. *The helmsman is at the wheel (left) and the top of the big after deckhouse is in front of him. The men look diminutive against the massive masts. She was built at Thomaston, Maine, in 1885 of 888 tons gross.* [W. J. LEWIS PARKER].

(Above) *The fore and main masts of the four-masted schooner* Andy Mahony *projecting out of a deck cargo of lumber. The chains passing over the lumber hold it firmly in place. This West Coast vessel was built in 1902 at Aberdeen, Washington, of 495 tons net.* [NATIONAL MARITIME MUSEUM, SAN FRANCISCO].

(Left) *In a fresh breeze, the crew are hauling in the jigger sheet of the four-masted schooner* Admiral. *She had a beam of 36.2 feet and a tonnage of 605, and was built at Coos Bay, Oregon, in 1899. Her deck cargo of lumber is in the foreground.* [NATIONAL MARITIME MUSEUM, SAN FRANCISCO].

massive multi-masted schooners which were equipped with four, five or six huge gaff sails. As owners called for larger hulls to meet the growing demand, shipwrights searched for new ways to bind together the enormous wooden hulls which sometimes exceeded 3000 tons. This shipbuilding programme became so extensive that it was not until 1894 that the tonnage of steamers in the coasting trade exceeded that of sailing vessels.

Ignoring the conversion of the steamer *Weybosset* into a four-masted schooner in 1879, the first real schooner on the East Coast to have four masts was the *William L. White* which was built in 1880. Describing her, Henry Hall wrote in his *Report of the Ship-building Industry of the United States* in 1882:

'The hull of the vessel was large enough for a Californian. She was 205 feet long on deck, 40 feet beam, and 17 feet deep in the hold, being 309 feet in length over all from the end of the jib-boom to the end of the spanker boom. She registered 996 tons, and

The Melrose *being towed down the Hoquiam River, Greys Harbour, Washington, by the tug* Traveler, *her decks piled high with lumber, and behind her are the dark pine woods which supplied the timber. Of 542 tons, she was built on this river in 1902. Captain Klebingat was her master in the 1920s when she traded between San Francisco and Pacific Islands.* [NATIONAL MARITIME MUSEUM, SAN FRANCISCO].

was able to carry 1,450 tons of anthracite coal. This vessel was rigged as a four-masted schooner. To have fitted her out with three masts would have required such large lower sails that the strain upon the masts would have been destructive, and she was therefore furnished with four, the after spar being called the spanker mast. This divided her 5,017 yards of canvas into smaller sails and made her a good schooner, sailing well, easily handled, and requiring a crew of only five men before the mast, besides her two mates and captain.'

The *William L. White* was built in 1880 at Bath, Maine, by Goss, Sawyer & Packard; after a brief career, she was lost at sea in November 1882. Henry Hall's description omits to state that the schooner had a centreboard. The remarkably small crew was only possible because of the steam donkey engine which provided power to handle speedily the heavy gear. Using steam power the *Josie R. Burt* hoisted all sail, excluding her topmast staysails, and hove in her anchor and thirty fathoms of chain in half-an-hour, while another schooner without a donkey engine took half-a-day to perform the same thing. Even in a gale, perhaps on a lee shore, steam could be raised and a schooner got underway by what would seem, on a square-rigger, to be a badly under-manned crew.

Like some of the large three-masters described in a previous chapter, many of the four-masters were flat-bottomed with moderately sharp ends and were particularly noticeable for their very pronounced sheer, raking stem, and the long bowsprit and jibboom from which five headsails were usually set. There was a gaff sail on each mast surmounted by a jib-headed topsail and on each topmast stay there was a large triangular staysail.

Coal was loaded at Philadelphia, Baltimore, Newport News or Norfolk for New

This fine picture of the crew 'taking the line' aboard the Sophie Christenson *presumably a towing line, was perhaps photographed from the tug after it had let go the hawser. The massive cathead is in the foreground and the big fore staysail is full of wind behind the crew which in 1913 numbered eighteen. She was built at Port Blakeley, Washington in 1901 of 570 tons.* [NATIONAL MARITIME MUSEUM, SAN FRANCISCO].

From the bowsprit looking aft aboard the six-masted schooner Edward B. Winslow. *On top of the forward deckhouse is the massive black-painted exhaust of the donkey engine which drove the halyard winches, pumps, windlass and cargo winches. The unbroken upper deck stretches away into the distance.* [PEABODY MUSEUM, SALEM].

York and Boston; other schooners might be carrying lumber from Maine or hard pine from the southern States, which meant filling the holds and then stacking it on the decks high above the bulwarks. A few schooners made ambitious voyages around Cape Horn or sailed to Australia, China and Europe.

It is recorded by Capt W. J. L. Parker in *The Great Coal Schooners of New England* how Albert Winslow of Taunton, Maine, designed the hulls of many famous schooners prior to 1890 and how he did this by carving a half-model; for this work which occupied him intermittently for between two and five weeks he was usually paid $100. In 1888, Albert Winslow suggested that the very large four-masted schooner proposed by Captain Davis be given a fifth mast. Thus was born the idea which resulted in the first five-master on the Atlantic coast, namely the *Governor Ames* of 1778 tons gross. She possessed a comparatively shallow-draft hull with a large centreboard case which greatly inconvenienced cargo handling but gave the needed stiffness for a large wooden hull.

The next five-master, the *Nathaniel T. Palmer*, was not launched for another ten years. Altogether fifty-six of them were built on the East Coast in the years 1888–1920 and the *Jane Palmer* at 3138 tons was the biggest. She was begun in 1902 as the six-master *Edward Burgess* and to have an auxiliary but instead was completed two years later as the five-master *Jane Palmer*.

The peak years for building multi-masted schooners, prior to the First World War were in the years 1898–1908. Included in this period was the production of all the ten six-masted schooners ever launched and also of the only seven-master. Howard I. Chapelle considered that these huge schooners were awkward to handle in confined waters and, because of their deficiency in longitudinal strength, could not be sailed really hard without becoming strained. The sheer size of the huge gaff sails made them very difficult to reef with such small crews, in spite of the invaluable donkey engine, and skippers had to gauge weather conditions carefully. Very few schooners were built of steel on the East Coast, largely because of cost, but important exceptions were the *Kineo* with five masts, built in 1903, and the six-master *William L. Douglas*.

On the Pacific Coast, 130 four-masted schooners were constructed in the years 1864 to 1904, but only one, the *Rosamund* (1900), was of over 1000 tons. Of the five-masters, only nine were built between 1888 and 1916 (inclusive). A yard was generally carried on the foremast for a square sail below it and triangular raffees above, but these were only set when the wind was abaft the beam. None of these vessels had centreboards. The late Dr. John Lyman contributed a valuable paper on the *Sailing*

This well-known view of the Edward B. Winslow *is one of the few shots ever taken of a deeply-laden schooner under full sail in a strong wind ploughing into the sea. This schooner measured 318.4ft × 50.0ft × 23.7ft, which was only 1.8ft shorter and 0.2ft narrower than the six masted schooner* Edward J. Lawrence *built the same year. Both had an identical beam, and were probably sisters, being both built for the same owner, J. S. Winslow & Co of Portland, Maine.* [PEABODY MUSEUM, SALEM].

Looking aloft on the six-masted schooner Mertie B. Crowley, *built 1907 of 2824 tons. On looking at this picture, Emmett A. Hoskins remarked: 'You can tell right away it's an East Coast schooner: there are no jigs [i.e. no tackles] on the halyards. Everything is hoisted by steam'. The topping lifts go to a double block shackled to the starboard trestletree. The jib-headed topsails are hooped to the masts like the gaff sails.* [NATIONAL MARITIME MUSEUM, SAN FRANCISCO].

Riding high in ballast, the steel-hulled Thomas W. Lawson *is under full sail with both topsails and staysails set, and the shadows cast make fascinating patterns. Her appearance is greatly improved if a piece of paper is laid lengthwise along the hull at an imaginary load line level. Her register length was 375.6 feet.* [PEABODY MUSEUM, SALEM].

The George W. Wells *was the first six-master built and was launched in 1900 with a gross tonnage of 2970 and a length of 319.3 ft. Some idea of the massive qualities of her enormous hull can be gained by studying the three levels of staging rigged along her sides, and the numbers of shipyard workers caulking her seams.* [PEABODY MUSEUM, SALEM].

Vessels of the Pacific Coast and their Builders which the Maritime Research Society of San Diego published as a bulletin subsequently to 1941.

There was a great boom in the second half of the First World War for building schooners owing to the shortage of tonnage. On the East Coast, this resulted in only a few five-masters being constructed but the number of four-masters increased dramatically, about 130 being built in the four years 1917–20, according to John Lyman's researches, published in *Log Chips*.

By contrast, the West Coast yards launched twenty-two five-masters in 1917 and fifty-seven the following year, according to Lyman's lists. Of four-masters, forty-one were built in these two years. Prior to the entry of America into the War in 1917, Norwegian owners had been ordering schooners; later America only allowed her Allies to order, and forty auxiliary steam schooners were built in Oregon and Washington in 1918 for the French Government. Most had short lives of only a few years and many were laid up in France.

In *Log Chips*, Dr. John Lyman has recorded that after the appearance of the

Shipping a sea abreast of the main rigging on the port side on the four-masted schooner Henry S. Little *which specialized in the coal, ice and phosphate trades. She was fitted with centreboards like many of her kind, having been built in 1889 at Bath, Maine, of 1096 tons gross.* [W. J. LEWIS PARKER].

The four-masted schooner Huntley *in frame and ready for planking at Scott's Bay, Nova Scotia, in 1918. Of 520 tons, she had a length of 175.8 ft. On ground covered with chips of wood, sawn timber has been laid out, and a pair of oxen are there to drag them to the sawpits or steam chest.* [PUBLIC ARCHIVES, NEW BRUNSWICK].

The four-masted schooner Cutty Sark *was built in 1919 at the end of the shipbuilding boom and she traded for ten years until abandoned on a passage from Nova Scotia to Bermuda. She measured 609 tons and is here shown with a big deck load of timber with stout vertical posts to prevent it shifting.* [NOVA SCOTIA MUSEUM, HALIFAX].

Interior of a cabin aboard the West Coast four-masted schooner Blakeley. [NATIONAL MARITIME MUSEUM, SAN FRANCISCO].

Aboard the five-masted schooner H. K. Hall *at the time of her launch in 1902 are her builder Henry K. Hall and his son James W. Hall. She registered 1105 net tons and was constructed at Port Blakeley, Washington.* [NATIONAL MARITIME MUSEUM, SAN FRANCISCO].

first six-masted schooners, seven and eight masts were being mentioned. The *Nautical Gazette* of December 1900 contained a proposal to build an eight-master of steel with dimensions of 400 ft × 52 ft × 30 ft. The following year, Bowdoin B. Crownin-shield designed one with seven masts and she was built of steel at Quincy, Massachusetts, and launched in 1902 with the name of *Thomas W. Lawson* measuring 375.6 ft × 50.0 ft × 22.9 ft and 5218 tons gross, and she once carried 9200 tons of coal on a draft of 30 feet. She was apparently operated successfully, first as a coal carrier, and later as an oil carrier; and in the latter trade, bound for London, she dragged ashore on the Scilly Isles in a gale in December 1907 and became a total loss. No other seven-master was built to replace her. Without any cargo aboard she was a difficult vessel to tack, especially in light winds, but when loaded she 'handled and steered nicely', according to her designer.

The last six-master afloat was the *Edward J. Lawrence* which was burned at Portland, Maine, on 27 December 1925, which meant that this breed of six-masters lasted a mere twenty-five years and yet this handful of schooners has always captured the imagination.

Most of Canada's four-masted schooners were built in the Maritime Provinces during the War and three registered over 1000 tons. The big schooners built in Europe are described in another chapter.

Altogether ten schooners were built with six masts on the East Coast. In order of launching they were:

name	year	tons gross	where built	builder	material
George W. Wells	1900	2970	Camden, Maine	H. M. Bean	wood
Eleanor A. Percy	1900	3402	Bath, Maine	Percy & Small	wood
Addie M. Lawrence	1902	2807	Bath, Maine	Percy & Small	wood
William L. Douglas	1903	3708	Quincy, Mass	Fore River S. B. Co	steel
Ruth E. Merrill	1904	3003	Bath, Maine	Percy & Small	wood
Alice M. Lawrence	1906	3132	Bath, Maine	Percy & Small	wood
Mertie B. Crowley	1907	2824	Rockland, Maine	Cobb, Butler & Co	wood
Edward J. Lawrence	1908	3350	Bath, Maine	Percy & Small	wood
Edward B. Winslow	1908	3424	Bath, Maine	Percy & Small	wood
Wyoming	1909	3730	Bath, Maine	Percy & Small	wood

This list appeared in *Log Chips* in July 1948.

Other vessels to be given six masts in the United States and rigged with fore-and-aft sails were the oil barge *Navahoe*, built in 1908 of 7718 tons, but always towed; the *Dovrefjeld* which was converted in 1917 from the ps *Rhode Island;* the *Katherine* ex *County of Linlithgow* (1887 of 2296 tons) was converted to a schooner in 1919 with auxiliary engines; and in 1920 three steamers were converted to the six-masted schooner rig. These last three were the *Oregon Fir* and *Oregon Pine*, both of 2526 tons and built of wood; and the *Fort Laramie* which had a Ferris-type hull. During World War II, two gambling barges which had been built as four-masted barques were rigged as bald-headed six-masted schooners at Los Angeles in 1941: the first was the *Star of Scotland* which was renamed *Ciudad Rodrigo;* the other was the *Mary Dollar* ex *Hans* which was renamed *Tango*. Two years later the barge-hulk of the old barque *Daylight* of 3756 tons was converted into a schooner in Puget Sound.

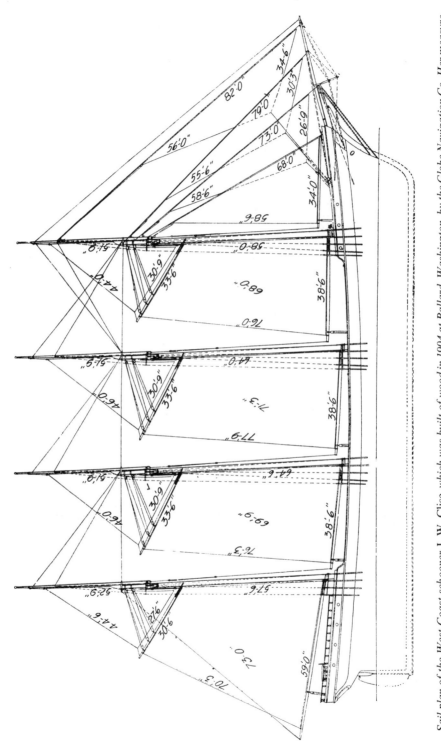

Sail plan of the West Coast schooner J. W. Clise which was built of wood in 1904 at Ballard, Washington, by the Globe Navigation Co. Her measurements were 185.6ft × 41.0ft × 14.0ft and 715 tons net. Printed in Marine Review April 1909. [NATIONAL MARITIME MUSEUM, SAN FRANCISCO].

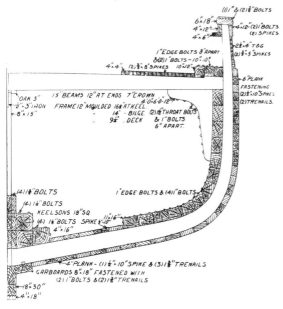

In a light breeze the Edward J. Lawrence *is running 'wing and wing' with the sail on the spanker mast boomed out to port to catch some more wind. The figure-of-eight shape taken up by most hulls is well illustrated in this picture. Her owners, J. S. Winslow & Co, owned twenty-one vessels in 1913 of which five were six-masted schooners; they also managed the Palmer Fleet consisting of twelve magnificent schooners.* [MARINERS MUSEUM].

Midship section of the four-masted schooner J. W. Clise *(1904). The massively built-up keelson and great thickness of the ceiling or inner planking are noteworthy to try and achieve longitudinal strength.* [NATIONAL MARITIME MUSEUM, SAN FRANCISCO].

CHAPTER FOURTEEN

Schooners Around the World

Due to American influence, the West Indies had a long tradition of building and operating schooners and the nature of the islands encouraged schooner traffic until recent times. As bases for privateers and pirates, the West Indies were ideal and reference has already been made to them on several occasions. Between the two World Wars, the schooners became run down and few new ones were built, but the creation of the Schooner Pool Authority in the British West Indies in 1942 stabilized things by creating work and organizing freights. The schooners had been fore-and-aft rigged for some years, and were mostly two-masters with a sprinkling of three masts. In 1921 a four-master of 696 tons, the *Marie J. Thompson*, was built in the Bahamas, presumably because of the high freight rates.

For Australia, the British Admiralty had designed a schooner in 1802 for use at Sydney, and schooners were in use as coastal and inter-island traders in the nineteenth and twentieth centuries. There was always a big fleet sailing to and from Tasmania

A pearling 'lugger' under sail off Australia's north-west coast with a Broome registration number on her bows. The masts seem of about equal height; there is no fore stay to the stem and a large jib is the only headsail. Average size is 45 to 65 ft. All the luggers now have auxiliary engines and are ketch rigged. In the 1880s they were lug-rigged but had the mizen set on a boom; the mizen was barely shorter than the mainmast. [E. K. PATTERSON].

Drying her sails in Sydney Harbour is the schooner Federal, *built at Balmain, N.S.W., in 1900 of 96 tons and registered at Sydney. The square sail from the foreyard may be bent to the yard. Many of the schooners here and in New Zealand were painted white.* [MacGREGOR COLLECTION].

The three-masted schooner Rahra, *built at Lake Macquarie, N.S.W., in 1912 originally traded between Melbourne and Hobart. By 1924 she had an auxiliary 40 HP engine and registered 93 tons gross with dimensions of 93.5 ft × 23.0 ft × 6.8 ft. About this time she worked the Ellice and Tokelau Islands, 5° to 10° S of the Equator, for Carruthers and Hedstrom.* [MacGREGOR COLLECTION].

and one of the last three-masted topsail schooners registered at Hobart was the *Alma Doepel*, built in 1903 but eventually cut down to a motor vessel.

Around New Zealand, schooners were in common use and Clifford Hawkins has recounted much of their history in the Auckland Province. Many fore-and-aft and topsail schooners were built to serve the isolated communities and to trade with some of the Pacific Islands. Some were lofty vessels with topgallant yards, and the regattas for commercial craft made imposing sights around the turn of the century.

The first scow or flat-bottomed barge with chines was the *Lake Erie* built in 1873, and by 1900 scows were very popular. Cargo was only carried on deck as the hull was about 5 feet deep, but centreboards were employed to make the hulls sail better to windward. Two and three-masted scows were constructed in addition to ketches, and the three-masters *Zingara* and *Pirate* had square topsails. Although sterns were square, the bows were often pointed with raking stems and of course carried bowsprits. The *Rangi* was the last scow to sail without auxiliary power as late as the 1930s.

Island schooners at Bequia in the Windward Islands. Their fore topmasts have veen removed and the craft on the right has been hove down to inspect her bottom. [R. A. CALVERT].

The American schooner Wanderer *at Shanghai c1865-70 drying her sails at anchor. She belonged to Augustine Heard & Co, the China merchants, but it is not known what her trade was.* [PEABODY MUSEUM, SALEM].

Presumably pilot cutter No 1 at anchor with her sails neatly furled in some hot climate, possibly the River Hooghly. The famous clipper Tweed *lies beyond, between her masts.* [MᴀᴄGREGOR COLLECTION].

Three local schooners at Mahé, in the Seychelle Islands, probably off the Long Pier at Port Victoria, with the rocky peaks behind. Sugar, tobacco and spices were exported in the nineteenth century. It is interesting to note the different rigs. [NEPTUNE PUBLICATIONS].

An unidentified schooner flying a pale blue flag bearing a white crescent moon which is probably Turkish. Painted in watercolour by R. H. Nibbs, it dates from c1815-45. The foremast is stepped very far up in the bows and the fore yard is placed well down the mast, requiring a deep roach to the topsail's foot. [PRIVATE COLLECTION].

CHAPTER FIFTEEN

Pilot Boats and Fishermen

In the British Isles, pilot cutters were rigged as fore-and-aft schooners at several places such as Fleetwood, Swansea and Liverpool. At Liverpool, the first of this rig was the *Pioneer* No 6 of 53 tons, built in 1852, and altogether there were sixteen schooners, the last being the clipper-bowed *George Holt* No 10, built in 1892 and sold in 1904. In *The Way of the World at Sea* (1896), W. J. Gordon writes:

'These Liverpool boats are reputed to be among the best afloat. They are good-sized schooners, averaging about seventy tons, roomy, fast, and weatherly, and able to keep the sea in all weathers. And it is very rough outside the Mersey bar on some occasions.'

The Mersey *on the stocks in 1875 at William Thomas' yard at Almwch, Anglsey, built for the Liverpool service. Of 79 tons she measured 80.7 ft × 19.0 ft × 10.8 ft.* [W. STEWART REES].

The Helen B. Thomas *was the first 'knockabout' fishing schooner and was built in 1902 at Essex without a bowsprit from a design by McManus.* [PEABODY MUSEUM, SALEM].

Racing for the Fisherman's Cup in 1931, the Gertrude L. Thebaud *of Gloucester (left) with an overall length of 134 ft 6 in, and the* Bluenose *with her 81 ft main boom. In this year,* Bluenose *won all three races. They again met in 1938 when* Bluenose *won three out of five races. The big four-sided or 'fisherman's' staysail set from the main topmast was typical of these schooners.* [NOVA SCOTIA MUSEUM, HALIFAX].

The Swansea pilot boats were smaller than these, probably being developed from a shallop, and they had a very raking mainmast. In the 1790s the schooners were small in size, 21 ft long and 6½ ft beam but were built larger from about 1860 and were decked over; by 1898 there were only two still in use.

On the Continent, the pilot schooners at Dunkirk and Bremerhaven resembled the Liverpool boats.

The Virginia pilot boat model has already been described and schooners were the

Many of the pilot schooners on the East Coast of the United States were splendid vessels with large suits of sails rather like some of the bigger fishing schooners. This one, the Adams, *was built at Essex, Massachusetts, in 1889 and was photographed by N. L. Stebbins in 1891. She looked similar to* Hesper No. 5. [PEABODY MUSEUM, SALEM].

The clipper-bowed fishing schooner Unique *was built at Essex, Massachusetts, in 1887 with dimensions of 74.2ft × 22.2ft × 8.5ft and a tonnage of 75 net. She could set a main gaff topsail, but no fore topmast was carried. Schooners of her type were popular in the mackerel fishery and in spite of their sharp lines were given heavy quarters to carry the huge mainsails then popular. They were broad in proportion to their length and of shallow draft compared with the Grand Bank schooners.* [PEABODY MUSEUM, SALEM].

recognized rig for American pilot boats. In the 1880s there were thirty schooners based on New York carrying pilots 600 miles out to sea in the search for ships. Many had vertical stems and were influenced by the fishing schooner as to rig but often discarded the fore topmast and so only carried two headsails.

The chebacco boats used for fishing off New England, as described in Chapter Four, were not large enough for the expanding fishing industry and the pinkies were not fast enough. Ports such as Essex and Gloucester began building 45-ton finer-lined schooners in the late 1830s, but fishing was by hand lines from the schooner's deck. Gradually larger boats evolved which resulted in the 'clipper' types of the late 1850s, an example of which was the *Flying Fish* of 1857 with an overall length of 74 feet and a beam of 21 feet, a long straight keel, hollow lines and clipper bow.

The yacht designer, Edward Burgess, introduced greater depth of hull and steeper deadrise into the *Carrie E. Phillips* in 1886, making her a big craft of 110 tons. The later curved stem became known as an 'Indian head' and was adopted by the whole Gloucester fleet. It was introduced by T. F. McManus about 1900. The 'knockabout' schooners of this period had no bowsprits but a longer and finely modelled hull.

A cup was donated in 1910 for the winner of the annual schooner races to be held at Digby, Nova Scotia, and this helped to promote continued interest in the schooners. Halifax and Lunenberg also built and owned many fishing schooners, and it was at the latter port that the celebrated *Bluenose* was launched in 1920. Racing continued during the 1930s and the last race was in 1938. A replica *Bluenose* was built in 1963.

Ships of many nationalities fished on the Grand Banks off Newfoundland and not least of these were the Portuguese who continued to send large schooners across the

The pinky Wave Queen *photographed in 1911 beside a wharf at Digby, Nova Scotia, on the Bay of Fundy. The peculiarity of this craft was her 'pink' stern in which the planking was cocked-up and run astern to enclose the rudder head. Her rig consisted of two pole masts setting gaff sails and a single headsail set on a bowsprit. They were used for inshore fishing up to the 1890s. The* Wave Queen *was built at St Andrews, N.B., in 1879 with dimensions of 30.2ft × 11.7ft × 5.1ft. I am grateful to Dr. Charles Armour for these particulars and for obtaining this print.* [FREDERICK WILLIAM WALLACE COLLECTION, MARITIME MUSEUM OF THE ATLANTIC, HALIFAX, N.S.].

Built at Oakland, California, in 1878 as a schooner yacht of 72 tons, the Casco *was chartered ten years later by Robert Louis Stevenson for a cruise in the South Seas. In her last days she operated as a sealer based at Victoria, British Columbia, in which capacity she was photographed here.* [NATIONAL MARITIME MUSEUM, SAN FRANCISCO].

A large four-masted schooner loading supplies at St John's, Newfoundland, in about 1948, prepara-tory to sailing for the cod-fishing grounds on the Grand Banks. Built of wood this schooner, although probably heavily-engined, still sets gaff sails on each mast as well as four headsails. In 1950, the Portuguese had six four-masted schooners built of wood in the Grand Banks fleet and this schooner was probably one of these. [NEPTUNE PUBLICATIONS].

Atlantic even after the Second World War. In 1966 there was a barquentine, six four-masted and two three-masted schooners in the trade. Not all had bowsprits but all had gaff sails and some also had fidded topmasts; all had powerful auxiliary engines. In 1936 the fleet had numbered fifty-seven of which only twenty-two were auxiliaries, and some were two-masted topsail schooners. In 1950, Alan Villiers sailed aboard the four-master *Argus* and immortalized her in his subsequent account of the voyage. In that year, apart from the trawlers and motor ships, there were thirty-one schooners, two of which had no engines at all, and one barquentine. The *Argus* was built of steel

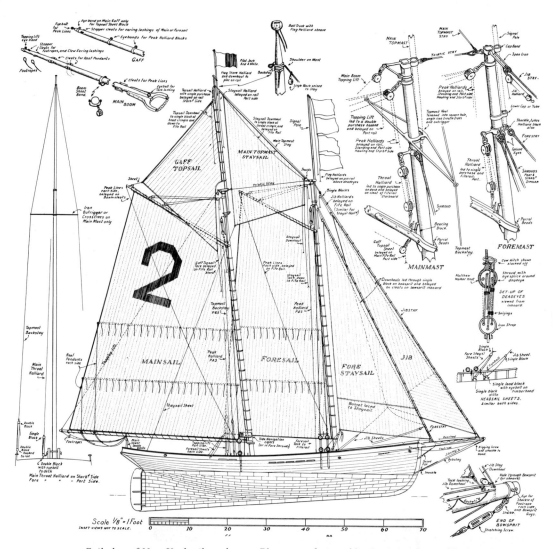

Sail plan of New York pilot schooner Phantom, *designed by D. J. Lawlor and built at East Boston in 1868 with dimensions of 76 ft 4 in (overall) × 19 ft 8 in × 19 ft 8 in (draft). As the fore topmast was only a light spar for displaying flags, neither flying jib nor gaff topsail could be carried, unlike the schooners of the 1890s. It seems odd that only two shrouds are fitted on the foremast and but a single one on the main, whereas the* Adams *of 1889 had three on each mast. Plan drawn by George F. Campbell.* [MODEL SHIPWAYS, BOGOTA, N. J.].

in Holland in 1938 with a tonnage of 696 and carried fifty-three dorymen. Schooners with tall topmasts set huge four-sided 'fisherman' staysails from the topmast stays when bound to or from the fishing grounds.

Schooners of any size seem to have been rarely used in the British Isles for fishing although the *Illustrated London News* reproduced an engraving in August 1851 of the *Spirit* of 116 tons which was built with three wet wells for carrying eels from Ireland and cod from Iceland. She had a straight stem and a lofty fore-and-aft rig. Another type, according to Roy Clark in *The Longshoremen*, was the Irish Wherry varying in size from 20 to 50 tons and employed at Skerries, just north of Dublin, in the first half of the nineteenth century. In appearance they resembled the Swansea pilot schooners with a straight stem, vertical foremast, markedly raked mainmast, but they had longer gaffs.

The French employed three-masted barquentines and a few big schooners to fish on the Grand Banks off Newfoundland and called them *terra-neuvas*. The two-masted schooners which they sent to fish for cod off Iceland were called *morutiers* and they were large vessels carrying a crew of twenty-six men; the hulls had deep heels and were really a modified version of a Gloucester fishing schooner. The cod were salted as soon as they were caught and to take them back to market another type of schooner was employed. This was the *chasseur* which had a crew of five or six and was designed to sail fast, resembling the *morutier* with a roller-reefing topsail but without the deep-heeled hull. These craft sailed down to Lisbon to load salt which they took up to Iceland to replenish the *morutiers*, taking in exchange the salted cod which they raced back to the French market.

Denmark had a few schooners fitted with wet wells to carry fish direct home from the fishing fleet.

Photographed at Bridgwater by W. A. Sharman, the King's Oak *is dried out and has staging hung over her sides for work to her planking. This schooner was built as a ketch at Great Yarmouth in 1884 by Fellows for fishing. The photograph shows she has fine lines with a bilge keel. In the 1890s she was lengthened by 15 feet so that she measured 88.2ft × 19.5ft × 9.4ft and 82 tons gross and was re-rigged as a schooner 'for fishing purposes' as the* Lloyd's Register *entry states, being then owned by Spillers & Bakers at Cardiff. She must have been almost unique in British waters unless she went deepsea.* [MacGREGOR COLLECTION].

CHAPTER SIXTEEN

School Ships

In the chronologically arranged list of vessels which Harold Underhill published in his *Sail Training and Cadet Ships* (1956), it is noteworthy that there were only four schooners used for training in the years 1838 to 1914, out of ninety-seven vessels listed. The emphasis in the world's maritime nations was still steadfastly fixed on square rig. The first schooner designed specifically for training purposes was the *Juan Sebastian de Elcano* which the Spanish Government had built in 1927 as a four-masted auxiliary of 3220 tons displacement. She set gaff sails on each mast as well as a topgallant on the foremast above double topsails.

Another large vessel was the Brazilian *Almirante Saldanha* of much the same size, but although having four 'schooner' masts, the fore gaff sail was replaced by staysails from the mainmast which makes her a sort of barquentine – possibly a schooner-bar-quentine on the same basis as the schooner-brigantines described in Chapter Seven.

With increasing costs, schooners became more popular from 1930 onwards. Two pairs of sister ships have visited many European harbours: the French *L'Étoile* and *La Belle Poule* were each built in 1932 with two masts and a roller-reefing topsail like the pre-War schooners from Brittany; and the Swedish *Gladan* and *Falkan* each built in 1947 with one yard for a square sail. All four are auxiliaries and built of steel. The two French schooners each carry thirty cadets, and the Swedes carry thirty-eight. Another cadet ship owned by Sweden from 1945–65 was the three-masted topsail schooner *Sunbeam II* which was renamed *Flying Clipper* in 1955.

The Danes built some sturdy wooden schooners for sail training such as the two-master *Lilla Dan* in 1951 and the three-master *Peder Most* which became *Prince Louis II* in 1955 when the Outward Bound Sea School at Burghead bought her. Most maritime nations acquired at least one school ship since World War II but it was no longer to train boys for commercial sailing ships. Training might be for the Navy or a shipping line or perhaps it might be more of the adventure type training. The British three-masted schooners *Sir Winston Churchill* and *Malcolm Miller* fit into the latter category with a permanent crew of about six and places for forty boys or girls.

The races amongst these school ships take place every two years and now a number of Baltic galleasses, converted into schooners or brigantines, carry some cadets so as to gain a place in one of these races. As a result, they and a few replica schooners of other days have been able to continue in a visual form the shapes of schooners from past epochs and, although sailing in ballast, their appearance has prompted some nostalgic memories amongst landlubbers and drawn some cryptic comments from old sailors.

The two-masted schooner Lilla Dan *under sail in Svendborg Sound in 1953. She was built two years earlier at Svendborg, Denmark, by J. Ring-Andersen for the Lauritzen Shipping Co and measured 120 tons with a length of 84.6 ft. The owner's insignia on the lower topsail is in red.* [AUTHOR].

Under sail aboard the Lilla Dan *in 1953 with a freshening breeze. The upper topsail has been furled and the two gaff sails reefed: the fore sail by rolling it round the boom; the main-sail by using reefing points.* [AUTHOR].

In Torbay August 1962, the day before the 'Tall Ships Race' began, one of the two French schooners– probably L'Etiole–*on the starboard tack. This schooner and her twin sister,* La Belle Poule, *were both built of steel in 1932 of 227 tons displace-ment and are still sailed by the French Navy. They are really copies of the topsail schooners sailing out of Brittany in the 1930s.* [PATRICIA M.A. GILPIN].

Built in 1932 as a gaff-rigged yacht, Brilliant *won the trans-Atlantic race to Plymouth the following year. In the 1950s she was given a tall Bermudian mainsail but retained her gaff foresail; in 1962 Captain 'Biff' Bowker took charge of her. Today she makes eighteen trips per year for the Mystic Seaport training project for teenagers. This photograph shows the 61-foot schooner leaving Latimer's Light astern in October 1977.* [M. A. STETS PHOTO, MYSTIC SEAPORT, CONN.].

The Polish training schooner Iskra, ex St Blane, ex Vlissingen *was built in 1917 in Holland and traded across the North Sea and English Channel until sold to Glasgow owners in 1925 and renamed St. Blane. Two years later she was sold to the Polish Government who ran her until the outbreak of war, when she was taken to Gibraltar for safety; but her fate is unknown.* [NEPTUNE PUBLICATIONS].

One of two three-masted schooners owned by the Sail Training Association of Great Britain, the Malcolm Miller *is here pictured off Great Yarmouth in 1979. She was built of steel in 1968 at Aberdeen with a gross tonnage of 219, an overall length of 150 ft and a maximum beam of 25 ft; height of mainmast above the deck is 97 ft 9 in. She has a permanent crew of six and can carry forty boys or girls. Her sister ship is the* Sir Winston Churchill *built two years earlier with the same length but 1 ft 8 in narrower.* [AUTHOR].

To replace the Prince Louis, *the Dulverton Trust built the three-masted topgallant yard schooner* Captain Scott *which was launched in 1970. She was built of larch on oak frames with steel deck beams by Herd & Mackenzie of Buckie with a length of 144 ft 3 in overall and a beam of 28 ft 0 in. Her rig is that of a typical merchant schooner such as the 'Western Ocean Yacht' category. She was sold about 1978 to interests in Oman for sail training at sea.* [NEPTUNE PUBLICATIONS].

The Peder Most, *nearest to the camera, racing with the* Lilla Dan *(seen under her bowsprit) in Svendborg Sound in 1953. The latter has a square sail set from her fore yard and also a main gaff topsail. The* Peder Most *was built of wood in 1944 for A. E. Sørensen of Svendborg with a tonnage of 160 and was at first named* Nette S. *In 1955 she was purchased by the Outward Bound Sea School at Burghead for about £11,500 and renamed* Prince Louis. *One of her commanders in this capacity was Cmdr Graham de Chair R.N. who tells me that she once made 18 knots for two hours when running for shelter before a force 8 gale. The School sold her in 1968 to the French organization Les Amis De Jeudi-Dimanche who renamed her* Bel Espoir. [F. HOLM-PETERSEN].

The Spanish four-masted schooner Juan Sebastian de Elcano *was built of steel at Cadiz in 1927 with auxiliary engines and is here seen at the start of the 'Tall Ships Race' off Boston in 1980. She has an overall length of 308 ft 9 in, a tonnage of 3750 and about 90 cadets. Here she is pointing right into the wind with the square sails aback.* [AUTHOR].

CHAPTER SEVENTEEN

Schooners Today

There is mounting enthusiasm today for the re-establishment of the classical rigs from the days of sail – brig, brigantine, barquentine, schooner, ketch and cutter, and all rigged with gaff sails rather than Bermudian. In the case of schooners, many are given one or more yards on the foremast so that the two and three-masted topsail schooner is once again sailing the seas. Some have been preserved such as the *Kathleen & May* by the Maritime Trust or the *Result* by the Ulster Folk Museum who lovingly maintain them afloat, their holds filled not with cargo, but with the relics and pictures of them and their contemporaries.

Unfortunately there are all too few of the genuine cargo-carrying schooners left because they were so neglected in hard times that they deteriorated beyond redemption although a few rigged down to motor ships have been rescued. Of this kind can be

The Aar *discharging at Teignmouth in 1960. Recently she was being converted to carry a larger sail area. She was built in 1932 as the* Patricia A. [MACGREGOR COLLECTION].

Seen at Wiscasset, Maine, in 1964 were the disintegrating hulls of two four-masters: the Hesper *(left) and the* Luther Little, *which had arrived there in 1932 and had waited ever since for cargoes.* [AUTHOR].

Many hulks of old sailing vessels have been broken up since the end of the last war, and Basil Green-hill and I watched this man smashing up the old timbers of the ketch Effort *at Galmpton on the River Dart in June 1952. This man had bought the remains of the* Effort *for £1.50. She was built at Kingsbridge in 1880 of 31 tons.* [AUTHOR].

Built in 1900 as the Lizzie May *and renamed* Kathleen & May *in 1908, this fine three-masted topsail schooner is today preserved by the Maritime Trust in St Katherine's Dock, London, where she was photographed in 1981 with the steam coaster* Robin *astern of her. The schooner was built by Ferguson & Baird at Connah's Quay, North Wales, of wood and measured 99 tons net and is said to have cost £2700. She is well worth a visit.* [AUTHOR].

Built in 1977, the Pride of Baltimore *is a faithful reproduction of the Baltimore clipper type and is owned and operated by the city of Baltimore. The fore topgallant has been sent down and the main gaff topsail is not set. She is steered with a tiller.* [AUTHOR].

cited the Australian three-master *Alma Doepel*, built in 1903 in New South Wales for inter-colonial trade, and still afloat in 1970 as a motor ship out of Hobart. In 1978 she was acquired by Sail & Adventure Ltd to be refitted, and perhaps the name of this organization epitomizes what many feel is the attraction to be found in schooners today. The three-masted topsail schooner *Aquila Marina*, which was built in Denmark in 1920, is another rescued vessel having been saved by the Grand Prix racing driver Jochen Mass from becoming a floating restaurant in Florida. Now she has been restored and sails in the Mediterranean.

Another cargo schooner to be reconstructed is the *Patricia A* . which was built of steel in Germany in 1932 with the name of *Aar*. She was fore-and-aft rigged only and continued trading until the late 1960s. In 1979 she was being refitted slowly on the Tyne at Newcastle as a fore-and-aft schooner with an enlarged sail area to trade in the West Indies, the idea being to make greater use of the wind as a motive power, and thereby economize in burning expensive fuel oil. Such a theme is being widely discussed at present and probably influences much of the restoration work in progress.

The use of newly-built schooners to carry cargo again is shared by a few enthusiasts and this notion was responsible for the construction of the two-masted centreboard schooner *John F. Leavitt* at Thomaston, Maine, in 1979. On a voyage to Haiti with a cargo of lumber she was abandoned on 28 December 1979 off Cape May, Delaware Bay, in bad weather with the vessel making water, and although the schooner was not actually seen to sink, no derelict has been found. No auxiliary engine was installed.

By far the largest proportion of schooners now afloat consists of vessels to be used for adventure cruises, for gaining experience under sail or for floating homes. In the pages of *Notices to Mariners International*, which is the journal of that organization and is edited by Erik Abranson, can be found much information on the numerous two, three and even four-masted schooners afloat today and what they are doing. It has provided many of the facts used here. But it is not all plain sailing today for the owners and their crews because not only foul weather takes its toll but also the growing activities of pirates which prey on defenceless vessels, just as they have done through the centuries.

On the opening page of his now classic book, *Wake of the Coasters*, the late John Leavitt wrote in 1970 that 'the dude cruisers are only maritime ghosts in an atomic world' and yet it looks as if their apparitions will increase to haunt us in the future.

Index

SHORT READING LIST

Charles A. Armour & Thomas Lackey, *Sailing Ships of the Maritimes* (1975).

William A. Baker, *Colonial Vessels* (1962).

Francis E. Bowker, *Hull-Down* (1963).

Robert Carse, *The Twilight of Sailing Ships* (1965).

Howard I. Chapelle, *The History of American Sailing Ships* (1935); *The National Watercraft Collection* [at Smithsonian Institution]; *American Sailing Craft* (1936); *The Search for Speed under Sail 1700–1855* (1967) .

Arthur H. Clark, *The History of Yachting* (1904).

B. B. Crowninshield, *Fore-and-Afters* (1940).

Basil Greenhill, *The Merchant Schooners* (2 vols, 1951 and 1957, but extensively revised 1968); *Schooners* (1980).

F. Holm-Petersen, *Maritime minder fra Marstal og Ærøskøbing* (1979) .

Garry J. Kerr, *Australian and New Zealand Sail Traders* (1974).

John Leather, *Gaff Rig* (1970).

John F. Leavitt, *Wake of the Coasters* (1970) .

John Lyman (editor), *Log Chips* (4 vols, 1948–59).

David R. MacGregor, *Fast Sailing Ships 1775–1875* (1973).

E. P. Morris, *The Fore-and-Rig in America* (1927).

John P. Parker, *Sails of the Maritimes* (1960).

W. J. Lewis Parker, *The Great Coal Schooners of New England 1870–1909* (1948).

Robert Simper, *Gaff Sail* (1979).